# The GDB Manual

The GNU Source-Level Debugger

Edition 4.03, for GDB Version 4.3
January 1992

## by Richard M. Stallman and Roland H. Pesch

Cover art by Etienne Suvasa.

# Lay Flat Binding

We have bound this manual using a new *lay-flat* binding technology. This type of binding allows you to open a soft cover book so that it "lays flat" on a table without creasing the binding.

In order to make the book lay flat properly, you need to "crack" the binding. To do this, divide the book into two sections and bend it so that the front and back covers meet. Do not worry; the pages are sewn and glued to the binding, and will not fall out easily. The outer cardboard binding itself is designed so that it will not break or crease as an ordinary paperback binding will. Bend the book several times in this manner, dividing it in a different place each time and pressing the pages flat and open. With use, the binding will become flexible and the pages will lay flat without needing to be pushed or held down.

# Short Contents

# Table of Contents

# Summary of GDB

The purpose of a debugger such as GDB is to allow you to see what is going on "inside" another program while it executes—or what another program was doing at the moment it crashed.

GDB can do four main kinds of things (plus other things in support of these) to help you catch bugs in the act:

- Start your program, specifying anything that might affect its behavior.
- Make your program stop on specified conditions.
- Examine what has happened, when your program has stopped.
- Change things in your program, so you can experiment with correcting the effects of one bug and go on to learn about another.

You can use GDB to debug programs written in C, C++, and Modula-2. Fortran support will be added when a GNU Fortran compiler is ready.

## Free Software

GDB is *free software*, protected by the GNU General Public License (GPL). The GPL gives you the freedom to copy or adapt a licensed program—but every person getting a copy also gets with it the freedom to modify that copy (which means that they must get access to the source code), and the freedom to distribute further copies. Typical software companies use copyrights to limit your freedoms; the Free Software Foundation uses the GPL to preserve these freedoms.

Fundamentally, the General Public License is a license which says that you have these freedoms and that you cannot take these freedoms away from anyone else.

For full details, see  [GNU GENERAL PUBLIC LICENSE], page 162.

## Contributors to GDB

Richard Stallman was the original author of GDB, and of many other GNU programs. Many others have contributed to its development. This section attempts to credit major contributors. One of the virtues of free software is that everyone is free to contribute to it; with regret, we cannot actually acknowledge everyone here. The file 'ChangeLog' in the GDB distribution approximates a blow-by-blow account.

Changes much prior to version 2.0 are lost in the mists of time.

*Plea:* Additions to this section are particularly welcome. If you or your friends (or enemies; let's be evenhanded) have been unfairly omitted from this list, we would like to add your names!

So that they may not regard their long labor as thankless, we particularly thank those who shepherded GDB through major releases: John Gilmore (all releases of GDB 4); Jim Kingdon (releases 3.9, 3.5, 3.4, 3.3); and Randy Smith (releases 3.2, 3.1, 3.0). As major maintainer of GDB for some period, each contributed significantly to the structure, stability, and capabilities of the entire debugger.

Richard Stallman, assisted at various times by Pete TerMaat, Chris Hanson, and Richard Mlynarik, handled releases through 2.8.

Michael Tiemann is the author of most of the GNU C++ support in GDB, with significant additional contributions from Per Bothner. James Clark wrote the GNU C++ demangler. Early work on C++ was by Peter TerMaat (who also did much general update work leading to release 3.0).

GDB 4 uses the BFD subroutine library to examine multiple object-file formats; BFD was a joint project of David V. Henkel-Wallace, Rich Pixley, Steve Chamberlain, and John Gilmore.

David Johnson wrote the original COFF support; Pace Willison did the original support for encapsulated COFF.

Adam de Boor and Bradley Davis contributed the ISI Optimum V support. Per Bothner, Noboyuki Hikichi, and Alessandro Forin contributed MIPS support. Jean-Daniel Fekete contributed Sun 386i support. Chris Hanson improved the HP9000 support. Noboyuki Hikichi and Tomoyuki Hasei contributed Sony/News OS 3 support. David Johnson contributed Encore Umax support. Jyrki Kuoppala contributed Altos 3068 support. Keith Packard contributed NS32K support. Doug Rabson contributed Acorn Risc Machine support. Chris Smith contributed Convex support (and Fortran debugging). Jonathan Stone contributed Pyramid support. Michael Tiemann contributed SPARC support. Tim Tucker contributed support for the Gould NP1 and Gould Powernode. Pace Willison contributed Intel 386 support. Jay Vosburgh contributed Symmetry support.

Rich Schaefer and Peter Schauer helped with support of SunOS shared libraries.

Jay Fenlason and Roland McGrath ensured that GDB and GAS agree about several machine instruction sets.

Patrick Duval, Ted Goldstein, Vikram Koka and Glenn Engel helped develop remote debugging. Intel Corporation and Wind River Systems contributed remote debugging modules for their products.

Brian Fox is the author of the readline libraries providing command-line editing and command history.

Andrew Beers of SUNY Buffalo wrote the language-switching code and the Modula-2 support, and contributed the Languages chapter of this manual.

# New Features since GDB Version 3.5

*Targets*    Using the new command `target`, you can select at runtime whether you are debugging local files, local processes, standalone systems over a serial port, realtime systems over a TCP/IP connection, etc. The command `load` can download programs into a remote system. Serial stubs are available for Motorola 680x0 and Intel 80386 remote systems; GDB also supports debugging realtime processes running under VxWorks, using SunRPC Remote Procedure Calls over TCP/IP to talk to a debugger stub on the target system. Internally, GDB now uses a function vector to mediate access to different targets; if you need to add your own support for a remote protocol, this makes it much easier.

*Watchpoints*

GDB now sports watchpoints as well as breakpoints. You can use a watchpoint to stop execution whenever the value of an expression changes, without having to predict a particular place in your program where this may happen.

*Wide Output*

Commands that issue wide output now insert newlines at places designed to make the output more readable.

*Object Code Formats*

GDB uses a new library called the Binary File Descriptor (BFD) Library to permit it to switch dynamically, without reconfiguration or recompilation, between different object-file formats. Formats currently supported are COFF, a.out, and the Intel 960 b.out; files may be read as .o's, archive libraries, or core dumps. BFD is available as a subroutine library so that other programs may take advantage of it, and the other GNU binary utilities are being converted to use it.

*Configuration and Ports*

Compile-time configuration (to select a particular architecture and operating system) is much easier. The script `configure` now allows you to configure GDB as either a native debugger or a cross-debugger. See Appendix D [Installing GDB], page 147, for details on how to configure and on what architectures are now available.

*Interaction*

The user interface to GDB's control variables has been simplified and consolidated in two commands, `set` and `show`. Output lines are now broken at readable places, rather than overflowing onto the next line. You can suppress output of machine-level addresses, displaying only source language information.

*C++*        GDB now supports C++ multiple inheritance (if used with a GCC version 2 compiler), and also has limited support for C++ exception handling, with the commands `catch` and `info catch`: GDB can break when an exception is raised, before the stack is peeled back to the exception handler's context.

*Modula-2*   GDB now has preliminary support for the GNU Modula-2 compiler, currently under development at the State University of New York at Buffalo. Coordinated development of both GDB and the GNU Modula-2 compiler will continue through the fall of 1991 and into 1992. Other Modula-2 compilers are currently not supported, and attempting to debug programs compiled with them will likely result in an error as the symbol table of the executable is read in.

*Command Rationalization*

Many GDB commands have been renamed to make them easier to remember and use. In particular, the subcommands of `info` and `show/set` are grouped to make the former refer to the state of your program, and the latter refer to the state of GDB itself. See Appendix C [Renamed Commands], page 145, for details on what commands were renamed.

*Shared Libraries*

GDB 4 can debug programs and core files that use SunOS shared libraries.

*Reference Card*

GDB 4 has a reference card. See Section D.4 [Formatting Documentation], page 152, for instructions on printing it.

*Work in Progress*

Kernel debugging for BSD and Mach systems; Tahoe and HPPA architecture support.

# 1  A Sample GDB Session

You can use this manual at your leisure to read all about GDB. However, a handful of commands are enough to get started using the debugger. This chapter illustrates these commands.

In this sample session, we emphasize user input like this: *input*, to make it easier to pick out from the surrounding output.

One of the preliminary versions of GNU m4 (a generic macro processor) exhibits the following bug: sometimes, when we change its quote strings from the default, the commands used to capture one macro's definition in another stop working. In the following short m4 session, we define a macro foo which expands to 0000; we then use the m4 built-in defn to define bar as the same thing. However, when we change the open quote string to <QUOTE> and the close quote string to <UNQUOTE>, the same procedure fails to define a new synonym baz:

```
$ cd gnu/m4
$ ./m4
define(foo,0000)

foo
0000
define(bar,defn('foo'))

bar
0000
changequote(<QUOTE>,<UNQUOTE>)

define(baz,defn(<QUOTE>foo<UNQUOTE>))
baz
C-d
m4: End of input: 0: fatal error: EOF in string
```

Let's use GDB to try to see what's going on.

```
$ gdb m4
GDB is free software and you are welcome to distribute copies
 of it under certain conditions; type "show copying" to see
 the conditions.
There is absolutely no warranty for GDB; type "show warranty"
 for details.
GDB 4.3, Copyright 1991 Free Software Foundation, Inc...
(gdb)
```

GDB reads only enough symbol data to know where to find the rest when needed; as a result, the first prompt comes up very quickly. We now tell GDB to use a narrower display width than usual, so that examples will fit in this manual.

```
(gdb) set width 70
```

Let's see how the m4 built-in changequote works. Having looked at the source, we know the relevant subroutine is m4_changequote, so we set a breakpoint there with GDB's break command.

```
(gdb) break m4_changequote
Breakpoint 1 at 0x62f4: file builtin.c, line 879.
```

Using the run command, we start m4 running under GDB control; as long as control does not reach the m4_changequote subroutine, the program runs as usual:

```
(gdb) run
Starting program: /work/Editorial/gdb/gnu/m4/m4
define(foo,0000)

foo
0000
```

To trigger the breakpoint, we call changequote. GDB suspends execution of m4, displaying information about the context where it stops.

```
changequote(<QUOTE>,<UNQUOTE>)

Breakpoint 1, m4_changequote (argc=3, argv=0x33c70)
    at builtin.c:879
879            if (bad_argc(TOKEN_DATA_TEXT(argv[0]), argc, 1, 3))
```

Now we use the command n (next) to advance execution to the next line of the current function.

```
(gdb) n
882            set_quotes((argc >= 2) ? TOKEN_DATA_TEXT(argv[1])\
 : nil,
```

set_quotes looks like a promising subroutine. We can go into it by using the command s (step) instead of next. step goes to the next line to be executed in any subroutine, so it steps into set_quotes.

```
(gdb) s
set_quotes (lq=0x34c78 "<QUOTE>", rq=0x34c88 "<UNQUOTE>")
    at input.c:530
530            if (lquote != def_lquote)
```

The display that shows the subroutine where m4 is now suspended (and its arguments) is called a stack frame display. It shows a summary of the stack. We can use the `backtrace` command (which can also be spelled `bt`), to see where we are in the stack as a whole: the `backtrace` command displays a stack frame for each active subroutine.

```
(gdb) bt
#0  set_quotes (lq=0x34c78 "<QUOTE>", rq=0x34c88 "<UNQUOTE>")
        at input.c:530
#1  0x6344 in m4_changequote (argc=3, argv=0x33c70)
        at builtin.c:882
#2  0x8174 in expand_macro (sym=0x33320) at macro.c:242
#3  0x7a88 in expand_token (obs=0x0, t=209696, td=0xf7fffa30)
        at macro.c:71
#4  0x79dc in expand_input () at macro.c:40
#5  0x2930 in main (argc=0, argv=0xf7fffb20) at m4.c:195
```

Let's step through a few more lines to see what happens. The first two times, we can use 's'; the next two times we use `n` to avoid falling into the `xstrdup` subroutine.

```
(gdb) s
0x3b5c  532             if (rquote != def_rquote)
(gdb) s
0x3b80  535             lquote = (lq == nil || *lq == '\0') ?  \
def_lquote : xstrdup(lq);
(gdb) n
536             rquote = (rq == nil || *rq == '\0') ? def_rquote\
 : xstrdup(rq);
(gdb) n
538             len_lquote = strlen(rquote);
```

The last line displayed looks a little odd; let's examine the variables `lquote` and `rquote` to see if they are in fact the new left and right quotes we specified. We can use the command `p` (`print`) to see their values.

```
(gdb) p lquote
$1 = 0x35d40 "<QUOTE>"
(gdb) p rquote
$2 = 0x35d50 "<UNQUOTE>"
```

`lquote` and `rquote` are indeed the new left and right quotes. Let's look at some context; we can display ten lines of source surrounding the current line, with the `l` (`list`) command.

```
(gdb) l
533             xfree(rquote);
534
```

```
535          lquote = (lq == nil || *lq == '\0') ? def_lquote\
  : xstrdup (lq);
536          rquote = (rq == nil || *rq == '\0') ? def_rquote\
  : xstrdup (rq);
537
538          len_lquote = strlen(rquote);
539          len_rquote = strlen(lquote);
540    }
541
542    void
```

Let's step past the two lines that set `len_lquote` and `len_rquote`, and then examine the values of those variables.

```
(gdb) n
539          len_rquote = strlen(lquote);
(gdb) n
540    }
(gdb) p len_lquote
$3 = 9
(gdb) p len_rquote
$4 = 7
```

That certainly looks wrong, assuming `len_lquote` and `len_rquote` are meant to be the lengths of `lquote` and `rquote` respectively. Let's try setting them to better values. We can use the `p` command for this, since it'll print the value of any expression—and that expression can include subroutine calls and assignments.

```
(gdb) p len_lquote=strlen(lquote)
$5 = 7
(gdb) p len_rquote=strlen(rquote)
$6 = 9
```

Let's see if that fixes the problem of using the new quotes with the `m4` built-in `defn`. We can allow `m4` to continue executing with the `c` (continue) command, and then try the example that caused trouble initially:

```
(gdb) c
Continuing.

define(baz,defn(<QUOTE>foo<UNQUOTE>))

baz
0000
```

Success! The new quotes now work just as well as the default ones. The problem seems to have been just the two typos defining the wrong lengths. We'll let **m4** exit by giving it an EOF as input.

C-d

`Program exited normally.`

The message '`Program exited normally.`' is from GDB; it indicates **m4** has finished executing. We can end our GDB session with the GDB `quit` command.

(gdb) quit

# 2  Getting In and Out of GDB

Type `gdb` or `gdb` *program core* to start GDB and type `quit` or `C-d` to exit.

## 2.1  Invoking GDB

Invoke GDB with the shell command `gdb`. Once started, GDB reads commands from the terminal until you tell it to exit.

You can run `gdb` with no arguments or options; but the most usual way to start GDB is with one argument or two, specifying an executable program as the argument:

    gdb *program*

You can also start with both an executable program and a core file specified:

    gdb *program core*

You can, instead, specify a process ID as a second argument, if you want to debug a running process:

    gdb *program* 1234

would attach GDB to process 1234 (unless you also have a file named '1234'; GDB does check for a core file first).

You can further control how GDB starts up by using command-line options. GDB itself can remind you of the options available.

Type

    gdb -help

to display all available options and briefly describe their use ('`gdb -h`' is a shorter equivalent).

All options and command line arguments you give are processed in sequential order. The order makes a difference when the '`-x`' option is used.

### 2.1.1  Choosing Files

When GDB starts, it reads any arguments other than options as specifying an executable file and core file (or process ID). This is the same as if the arguments were specified by the '`-se`' and '`-c`' options respectively. (GDB reads the first argument that does not have an associated option flag as equivalent to the '`-se`' option followed by that argument; and the second argument that does not have an associated option flag, if any, as equivalent to the '`-c`' option followed by that argument.)

Many options have both long and short forms; both are shown in the following list. GDB also recognizes the long forms if you truncate them, so long as enough of the option is present to be unambiguous. (If you prefer, you can flag option arguments with '--' rather than '-', though we illustrate the more usual convention.)

**-symbols=***file*
**-s** *file*      Read symbol table from file *file*.

**-exec=***file*
**-e** *file*      Use file *file* as the executable file to execute when appropriate, and for examining pure data in conjunction with a core dump.

**-se=***file*      Read symbol table from file *file* and use it as the executable file.

**-core=***file*
**-c** *file*      Use file *file* as a core dump to examine.

**-command=***file*
**-x** *file*      Execute GDB commands from file *file*. See Section 15.2 [Command Files], page 120.

**-directory=***directory*
**-d** *directory*

      Add *directory* to the path to search for source files.

## 2.1.2 Choosing Modes

You can run GDB in various alternative modes—for example, in batch mode or quiet mode.

**-nx**
**-n**      Do not execute commands from any '.gdbinit' initialization files. Normally, the commands in these files are executed after all the command options and arguments have been processed. See Section 15.2 [Command Files], page 120.

**-quiet**
**-q**      "Quiet". Do not print the introductory and copyright messages. These messages are also suppressed in batch mode.

**-batch**      Run in batch mode. Exit with status 0 after processing all the command files specified with '-x' (and '.gdbinit', if not inhibited). Exit with nonzero status if an error occurs in executing the GDB commands in the command files.

      Batch mode may be useful for running GDB as a filter, for example to download and run a program on another computer; in order to make this more useful, the message

> Program exited normally.

> (which is ordinarily issued whenever a program running under GDB control terminates) is not issued when running in batch mode.

**-cd=***directory*

> Run GDB using *directory* as its working directory, instead of the current directory.

**-fullname**

**-f**

> Emacs sets this option when it runs GDB as a subprocess. It tells GDB to output the full file name and line number in a standard, recognizable fashion each time a stack frame is displayed (which includes each time your program stops). This recognizable format looks like two '\032' characters, followed by the file name, line number and character position separated by colons, and a newline. The Emacs-to-GDB interface program uses the two '\032' characters as a signal to display the source code for the frame.

**-b** *bps*

> Set the line speed (baud rate or bits per second) of any serial interface used by GDB for remote debugging.

**-tty=***device*

> Run using *device* for your program's standard input and output.

## 2.2  Quitting GDB

**quit**     To exit GDB, use the **quit** command (abbreviated q), or type an end-of-file character (usually C-d).

An interrupt (often C-c) will not exit from GDB, but rather will terminate the action of any GDB command that is in progress and return to GDB command level. It is safe to type the interrupt character at any time because GDB does not allow it to take effect until a time when it is safe.

If you have been using GDB to control an attached process or device, you can release it with the **detach** command; see Section 4.7 [Debugging an Already-Running Process], page 26.

## 2.3  Shell Commands

If you need to execute occasional shell commands during your debugging session, there is no need to leave or suspend GDB; you can just use the **shell** command.

`shell` *command string*

> Directs GDB to invoke an inferior shell to execute *command string*. If it exists, the environment variable `SHELL` is used for the name of the shell to run. Otherwise GDB uses `/bin/sh`.

The utility **make** is often needed in development environments. You do not have to use the **shell** command for this purpose in GDB:

**make** *make-args*

> Causes GDB to execute an inferior **make** program with the specified arguments. This is equivalent to '**shell make** *make-args*'.

# 3  GDB Commands

You can abbreviate a GDB command if that abbreviation is unambiguous; and you can repeat certain GDB commands by typing just RET.

## 3.1  Command Syntax

A GDB command is a single line of input. There is no limit on how long it can be. It starts with a command name, which is followed by arguments whose meaning depends on the command name. For example, the command step accepts an argument which is the number of times to step, as in 'step 5'. You can also use the step command with no arguments. Some command names do not allow any arguments.

GDB command names may always be truncated if that abbreviation is unambiguous. Other possible command abbreviations are listed in the documentation for individual commands. In some cases, even ambiguous abbreviations are allowed; for example, s is specially defined as equivalent to step even though there are other commands whose names start with s. You can test abbreviations by using them as arguments to the help command.

A blank line as input to GDB (typing just RET) means to repeat the previous command. Certain commands (for example, run) will not repeat this way; these are commands for which unintentional repetition might cause trouble and which you are unlikely to want to repeat.

The list and x commands, when you repeat them with RET, construct new arguments rather than repeating exactly as typed. This permits easy scanning of source or memory.

GDB can also use RET in another way: to partition lengthy output, in a way similar to the common utility more (see Section 14.4 [Screen Size], page 115). Since it is easy to press one RET too many in this situation, GDB disables command repetition after any command that generates this sort of display.

A line of input starting with # is a comment; it does nothing. This is useful mainly in command files (see Section 15.2 [Command Files], page 120).

## 3.2  Getting Help

You can always ask GDB itself for information on its commands, using the command help.

help
h           You can use help (abbreviated h) with no arguments to display
            a short list of named classes of commands:

```
(gdb) help
List of classes of commands:

running -- Running the program
stack -- Examining the stack
data -- Examining data
breakpoints -- Making program stop at certain points
files -- Specifying and examining files
status -- Status inquiries
support -- Support facilities
user-defined -- User-defined commands
aliases -- Aliases of other commands
obscure -- Obscure features

Type "help" followed by a class name for a list of
commands in that class.
Type "help" followed by command name for full
documentation.
Command name abbreviations are allowed if unambiguous.
(gdb)
```

help *class*  Using one of the general help classes as an argument, you can
            get a list of the individual commands in that class. For example,
            here is the help display for the class status:

```
(gdb) help status
Status inquiries.

List of commands:

show -- Generic command for showing things set with "set"
info -- Generic command for printing status

Type "help" followed by command name for full
documentation.
Command name abbreviations are allowed if unambiguous.
(gdb)
```

help *command*

            With a command name as help argument, GDB will display a
            short paragraph on how to use that command.

In addition to `help`, you can use the GDB commands `info` and `show` to inquire about the state of your program, or the state of GDB itself. Each command supports many topics of inquiry; this manual introduces each of them in the appropriate context. The listings under `info` and under `show` in the Index point to all the sub-commands. See [Index], page 165.

info
: This command (abbreviated `i`) is for describing the state of your program. For example, you can list the arguments given to your program with `info args`, list the registers currently in use with `info registers`, or list the breakpoints you have set with `info breakpoints`. You can get a complete list of the `info` sub-commands with `help info`.

show
: In contrast, `show` is for describing the state of GDB itself. You can change most of the things you can `show`, by using the related command `set`; for example, you can control what number system is used for displays with `set radix`, or simply inquire which is currently in use with `show radix`.

 To display all the settable parameters and their current values, you can use `show` with no arguments; you may also use `info set`. Both commands produce the same display.

Here are three miscellaneous `show` subcommands, all of which are exceptional in lacking corresponding `set` commands:

show version
: Show what version of GDB is running. You should include this information in GDB bug-reports. If multiple versions of GDB are in use at your site, you may occasionally want to determine which version of GDB you are running; as GDB evolves, new commands are introduced, and old ones may wither away. The version number is also announced when you start GDB with no arguments.

show copying
: Display information about permission for copying GDB.

show warranty
: Display the GNU "NO WARRANTY" statement.

# 4  Running Programs Under GDB

When you run a program under GDB, you must first generate debugging information for it when you compile it. You may start it with its arguments, if any, in an environment of your choice. You may redirect your program's input and output, debug an already running process, or kill a child process.

## 4.1  Compiling for Debugging

In order to debug a program effectively, you need to generate debugging information when you compile it. This debugging information is stored in the object file; it describes the data type of each variable or function and the correspondence between source line numbers and addresses in the executable code.

To request debugging information, specify the '-g' option when you run the compiler.

Many C compilers are unable to handle the '-g' and '-O' options together. Using those compilers, you cannot generate optimized executables containing debugging information.

The GNU C compiler supports '-g' with or without '-O', making it possible to debug optimized code. We recommend that you *always* use '-g' whenever you compile a program. You may think your program is correct, but there is no sense in pushing your luck.

Some things do not work as well with '-g -O' as with just '-g', particularly on machines with instruction scheduling. If in doubt, recompile with '-g' alone, and if this fixes the problem, please report it as a bug (including a test case!).

Older versions of the GNU C compiler permitted a variant option '-gg' for debugging information. GDB no longer supports this format; if your GNU C compiler has this option, do not use it.

## 4.2  Starting your Program

run
r

Use the run command to start your program under GDB. You must first specify the program name (except on VxWorks) with an argument to GDB (see Chapter 2 [Getting In and Out of GDB], page 13), or by using the file or exec-file command (see Section 12.1 [Commands to Specify Files], page 97).

If you are running your program in an execution environment that supports processes, **run** creates an inferior process and makes that process run your program. (In environments without processes, **run** jumps to the start of your program.)

The execution of a program is affected by certain information it receives from its superior. GDB provides ways to specify this information, which you must do *before* starting your program. (You can change it after starting your program, but such changes will only affect your program the next time you start it.) This information may be divided into four categories:

The *arguments*.

> Specify the arguments to give your program as the arguments of the **run** command. If a shell is available on your target, the shell is used to pass the arguments, so that you may use normal conventions (such as wildcard expansion or variable substitution) in describing the arguments. In Unix systems, you can control which shell is used with the **SHELL** environment variable. See Section 4.3 [Your Program's Arguments], page 23.

The *environment*.

> Your program normally inherits its environment from GDB, but you can use the GDB commands **set environment** and **unset environment** to change parts of the environment that will be given to your program. See Section 4.4 [Your Program's Environment], page 23.

The *working directory*.

> Your program inherits its working directory from GDB. You can set GDB's working directory with the **cd** command in GDB. See Section 4.5 [Your Program's Working Directory], page 24.

The *standard input and output*.

> Your program normally uses the same device for standard input and standard output as GDB is using. You can redirect input and output in the **run** command line, or you can use the **tty** command to set a different device for your program. See Section 4.6 [Your Program's Input and Output], page 25.

> *Warning:* While input and output redirection work, you cannot use pipes to pass the output of the program you are debugging to another program; if you attempt this, GDB is likely to wind up debugging the wrong program.

When you issue the **run** command, your program begins to execute immediately. See Chapter 5 [Stopping and Continuing], page 29, for discussion of how to arrange for your program to stop. Once your program has been started by the `run` command (and then stopped), you may evaluate expressions that involve calls to functions in your program, using the `print` or `call` commands. See Chapter 8 [Examining Data], page 57.

If the modification time of your symbol file has changed since the last time GDB read its symbols, GDB will discard its symbol table and re-read it. When it does this, GDB tries to retain your current breakpoints.

## 4.3  Your Program's Arguments

The arguments to your program can be specified by the arguments of the `run` command. They are passed to a shell, which expands wildcard characters and performs redirection of I/O, and thence to your program. GDB uses the shell indicated by your `SHELL` environment variable if it exists; otherwise, GDB uses `/bin/sh`.

`run` with no arguments uses the same arguments used by the previous `run`, or those set by the `set args` command.

set args    Specify the arguments to be used the next time your program is run. If `set args` has no arguments, `run` will execute your program with no arguments. Once you have run your program with arguments, using `set args` before the next `run` is the only way to run it again without arguments.

show args   Show the arguments to give your program when it is started.

## 4.4  Your Program's Environment

The *environment* consists of a set of environment variables and their values. Environment variables conventionally record such things as your user name, your home directory, your terminal type, and your search path for programs to run. Usually you set up environment variables with the shell and they are inherited by all the other programs you run. When debugging, it can be useful to try running your program with a modified environment without having to start GDB over again.

path *directory*

Add *directory* to the front of the `PATH` environment variable (the search path for executables), for both GDB and your program. You may specify several directory names, separated by ':' or whitespace. If *directory* is already in the path, it is moved to the front, so it will be searched sooner.

You can use the string '$cwd' to refer to whatever is the current working directory at the time GDB searches the path. If you use '.' instead, it refers to the directory where you executed the path command. GDB fills in the current path where needed in the *directory* argument, before adding it to the search path.

show paths

Display the list of search paths for executables (the PATH environment variable).

show environment [*varname*]

Print the value of environment variable *varname* to be given to your program when it starts. If you do not supply *varname*, print the names and values of all environment variables to be given to your program. You can abbreviate environment as env.

set environment *varname* [=] *value*

Set environment variable *varname* to *value*. The value changes for your program only, not for GDB itself. *value* may be any string; the values of environment variables are just strings, and any interpretation is supplied by your program itself. The *value* parameter is optional; if it is eliminated, the variable is set to a null value.

For example, this command:

```
set env USER = foo
```

tells a Unix program, when subsequently run, that its user is named 'foo'. (The spaces around '=' are used for clarity here; they are not actually required.)

unset environment *varname*

Remove variable *varname* from the environment to be passed to your program. This is different from 'set env *varname* ='; unset environment removes the variable from the environment, rather than assigning it an empty value.

## 4.5  Your Program's Working Directory

Each time you start your program with run, it inherits its working directory from the current working directory of GDB. GDB's working directory is initially whatever it inherited from its parent process (typically the shell), but you can specify a new working directory in GDB with the cd command.

The GDB working directory also serves as a default for the commands that specify files for GDB to operate on.  See Section 12.1 [Commands to Specify Files], page 97.

cd *directory*

> Set GDB's working directory to *directory*.

pwd

> Print GDB's working directory.

## 4.6 Your Program's Input and Output

By default, the program you run under GDB does input and output to the same terminal that GDB uses.  GDB switches the terminal to its own terminal modes to interact with you, but it records the terminal modes your program was using and switches back to them when you continue running your program.

info terminal

> Displays GDB's recorded information about the terminal modes your program is using.

You can redirect your program's input and/or output using shell redirection with the run command. For example,

    run > outfile

starts your program, diverting its output to the file 'outfile'.

Another way to specify where your program should do input and output is with the tty command. This command accepts a file name as argument, and causes this file to be the default for future run commands. It also resets the controlling terminal for the child process, for future run commands. For example,

    tty /dev/ttyb

directs that processes started with subsequent run commands default to do input and output on the terminal '/dev/ttyb' and have that as their controlling terminal.

An explicit redirection in run overrides the tty command's effect on the input/output device, but not its effect on the controlling terminal.

When you use the tty command or redirect input in the run command, only the input *for your program* is affected. The input for GDB still comes from your terminal.

## 4.7  Debugging an Already-Running Process

attach *process-id*

> This command attaches to a running process—one that was
> started outside GDB. (info files will show your active tar-
> gets.) The command takes as argument a process ID. The usual
> way to find out the process-id of a Unix process is with the ps
> utility, or with the 'jobs -l' shell command.
>
> attach will not repeat if you press RET a second time after exe-
> cuting the command.

To use attach, you must be debugging in an environment which supports
processes. You must also have permission to send the process a signal, and
it must have the same effective user ID as the GDB process.

When using attach, you should first use the file command to specify the
program running in the process and load its symbol table. See Section 12.1
[Commands to Specify Files], page 97.

The first thing GDB does after arranging to debug the specified process
is to stop it. You can examine and modify an attached process with all the
GDB commands that are ordinarily available when you start processes with
run. You can insert breakpoints; you can step and continue; you can modify
storage. If you would rather the process continue running, you may use the
continue command after attaching GDB to the process.

detach

> When you have finished debugging the attached process, you
> can use the detach command to release it from GDB's control.
> Detaching the process continues its execution. After the detach
> command, that process and GDB become completely indepen-
> dent once more, and you are ready to attach another process
> or start one with run. detach will not repeat if you press RET
> again after executing the command.

If you exit GDB or use the run command while you have an attached
process, you kill that process. By default, you will be asked for confirmation
if you try to do either of these things; you can control whether or not you need
to confirm by using the set confirm command (see Section 14.6 [Optional
Warnings and Messages], page 116).

## 4.8  Killing the Child Process

kill

> Kill the child process in which your program is running under
> GDB.

This command is useful if you wish to debug a core dump instead of a running process. GDB ignores any core dump file while your program is running.

On some operating systems, a program cannot be executed outside GDB while you have breakpoints set on it inside GDB. You can use the `kill` command in this situation to permit running your program outside the debugger.

The `kill` command is also useful if you wish to recompile and relink your program, since on many systems it is impossible to modify an executable file while it is running in a process. In this case, when you next type `run`, GDB will notice that the file has changed, and will re-read the symbol table (while trying to preserve your current breakpoint settings).

# 5  Stopping and Continuing

The principal purposes of using a debugger are so that you can stop your program before it terminates; or so that, if your program runs into trouble, you can investigate and find out why.

Inside GDB, your program may stop for any of several reasons, such as a signal, a breakpoint, or reaching a new line after a GDB command such as `step`. You may then examine and change variables, set new breakpoints or remove old ones, and then continue execution. Usually, the messages shown by GDB provide ample explanation of the status of your program—but you can also explicitly request this information at any time.

`info program`

> Display information about the status of your program: whether it is running or not, what process it is, and why it stopped.

## 5.1  Breakpoints, Watchpoints, and Exceptions

A *breakpoint* makes your program stop whenever a certain point in the program is reached. For each breakpoint, you can add various conditions to control in finer detail whether your program will stop. You can set breakpoints with the `break` command and its variants (see Section 5.1.1 [Setting Breakpoints], page 30), to specify the place where your program should stop by line number, function name or exact address in the program. In languages with exception handling (such as GNU C++), you can also set breakpoints where an exception is raised (see Section 5.1.3 [Breakpoints and Exceptions], page 32).

A *watchpoint* is a special breakpoint that stops your program when the value of an expression changes. You must use a different command to set watchpoints (see Section 5.1.2 [Setting Watchpoints], page 32), but aside from that, you can manage a watchpoint like any other breakpoint: you enable, disable, and delete both breakpoints and watchpoints using the same commands.

Each breakpoint or watchpoint is assigned a number when it is created; these numbers are successive integers starting with one. In many of the commands for controlling various features of breakpoints you use the breakpoint number to say which breakpoint you want to change. Each breakpoint may be *enabled* or *disabled*; if disabled, it has no effect on your program until you enable it again.

### 5.1.1  Setting Breakpoints

Breakpoints are set with the `break` command (abbreviated `b`).

You have several ways to say where the breakpoint should go.

`break` *function*

> Set a breakpoint at entry to function *function*. When using source languages that permit overloading of symbols, such as C++, *function* may refer to more than one possible place to break. See Section 5.1.8 [Breakpoint Menus], page 39, for a discussion of that situation.

`break +`*offset*
`break -`*offset*

> Set a breakpoint some number of lines forward or back from the position at which execution stopped in the currently selected frame.

`break` *linenum*

> Set a breakpoint at line *linenum* in the current source file. That file is the last file whose source text was printed. This breakpoint will stop your program just before it executes any of the code on that line.

`break` *filename*`:`*linenum*

> Set a breakpoint at line *linenum* in source file *filename*.

`break` *filename*`:`*function*

> Set a breakpoint at entry to function *function* found in file *filename*. Specifying a file name as well as a function name is superfluous except when multiple files contain similarly named functions.

`break *`*address*

> Set a breakpoint at address *address*. You can use this to set breakpoints in parts of your program which do not have debugging information or source files.

`break`

> When called without any arguments, `break` sets a breakpoint at the next instruction to be executed in the selected stack frame (see Chapter 6 [Examining the Stack], page 45). In any selected frame but the innermost, this will cause your program to stop as soon as control returns to that frame. This is similar to the effect of a `finish` command in the frame inside the selected frame—except that `finish` does not leave an active breakpoint. If you use `break` without an argument in the innermost frame,

GDB will stop the next time it reaches the current location; this may be useful inside loops.

GDB normally ignores breakpoints when it resumes execution, until at least one instruction has been executed. If it did not do this, you would be unable to proceed past a breakpoint without first disabling the breakpoint. This rule applies whether or not the breakpoint already existed when your program stopped.

**break ... if** *cond*

Set a breakpoint with condition *cond*; evaluate the expression *cond* each time the breakpoint is reached, and stop only if the value is nonzero—that is, if *cond* evaluates as true. '...' stands for one of the possible arguments described above (or no argument) specifying where to break. See Section 5.1.6 [Break Conditions], page 35, for more information on breakpoint conditions.

**tbreak** *args*

Set a breakpoint enabled only for one stop. *args* are the same as for the **break** command, and the breakpoint is set in the same way, but the breakpoint is automatically disabled after the first time your program stops there. See Section 5.1.5 [Disabling Breakpoints], page 34.

**rbreak** *regex*

Set breakpoints on all functions matching the regular expression *regex*. This command sets an unconditional breakpoint on all matches, printing a list of all breakpoints it set. Once these breakpoints are set, they are treated just like the breakpoints set with the **break** command. They can be deleted, disabled, made conditional, etc., in the standard ways.

When debugging C++ programs, **rbreak** is useful for setting breakpoints on overloaded functions that are not members of any special classes.

**info breakpoints** [*n*]

**info break** [*n*]

Print a list of all breakpoints (but not watchpoints) set and not deleted, showing their numbers, where in your program they are, and any special features in use for them. Disabled breakpoints are included in the list, but marked as disabled. **info break** with a breakpoint number *n* as argument lists only that breakpoint. The convenience variable $_ and the default examining-address for the x command are set to the address of the last breakpoint listed (see Section 8.5 [Examining Memory], page 61). The equivalent command for watchpoints is `info watch`.

GDB allows you to set any number of breakpoints at the same place in your program. There is nothing silly or meaningless about this. When the breakpoints are conditional, this is even useful (see Section 5.1.6 [Break Conditions], page 35).

## 5.1.2  Setting Watchpoints

You can use a watchpoint to stop execution whenever the value of an expression changes, without having to predict a particular place where this may happen.

Watchpoints currently execute two orders of magnitude more slowly than other breakpoints, but this can well be worth it to catch errors where you have no clue what part of your program is the culprit. Some processors provide special hardware to support watchpoint evaluation; future releases of GDB will use such hardware if it is available.

watch *expr*

> Set a watchpoint for an expression.

info watchpoints

> This command prints a list of watchpoints; it is otherwise similar to `info break`.

## 5.1.3  Breakpoints and Exceptions

Some languages, such as GNU C++, implement exception handling. You can use GDB to examine what caused your program to raise an exception, and to list the exceptions your program is prepared to handle at a given point in time.

catch *exceptions*

> You can set breakpoints at active exception handlers by using the `catch` command. *exceptions* is a list of names of exceptions to catch.

You can use `info catch` to list active exception handlers. See Section 6.4 [Information About a Frame], page 48.

There are currently some limitations to exception handling in GDB. These will be corrected in a future release.

- If you call a function interactively, GDB normally returns control to you when the function has finished executing. If the call raises an exception, however, the call may bypass the mechanism that returns control to you and cause your program to simply continue running until it hits a breakpoint, catches a signal that GDB is listening for, or exits.

- You cannot raise an exception interactively.

- You cannot interactively install an exception handler.

Sometimes `catch` is not the best way to debug exception handling: if you need to know exactly where an exception is raised, it is better to stop *before* the exception handler is called, since that way you can see the stack before any unwinding takes place. If you set a breakpoint in an exception handler instead, it may not be easy to find out where the exception was raised.

To stop just before an exception handler is called, you need some knowledge of the implementation. In the case of GNU C++, exceptions are raised by calling a library function named `__raise_exception` which has the following ANSI C interface:

```
/* addr is where the exception identifier is stored.
   ID is the exception identifier.  */
void __raise_exception (void **addr, void *id);
```

To make the debugger catch all exceptions before any stack unwinding takes place, set a breakpoint on `__raise_exception` (see Section 5.1 [Breakpoints Watchpoints and Exceptions], page 29).

With a conditional breakpoint (see Section 5.1.6 [Break Conditions], page 35) that depends on the value of *id*, you can stop your program when a specific exception is raised. You can use multiple conditional breakpoints to stop your program when any of a number of exceptions are raised.

## 5.1.4  Deleting Breakpoints

It is often necessary to eliminate a breakpoint or watchpoint once it has done its job and you no longer want your program to stop there. This is called *deleting* the breakpoint. A breakpoint that has been deleted no longer exists; it is forgotten.

With the `clear` command you can delete breakpoints according to where they are in your program. With the `delete` command you can delete individual breakpoints or watchpoints by specifying their breakpoint numbers.

It is not necessary to delete a breakpoint to proceed past it. GDB automatically ignores breakpoints on the first instruction to be executed when you continue execution without changing the execution address.

clear            Delete any breakpoints at the next instruction to be executed
                 in the selected stack frame (see Section 6.3 [Selecting a Frame],
                 page 47). When the innermost frame is selected, this is a good
                 way to delete a breakpoint where your program just stopped.

clear *function*
clear *filename*:*function*
                 Delete any breakpoints set at entry to the function *function*.

clear *linenum*
clear *filename*:*linenum*
                 Delete any breakpoints set at or within the code of the specified
                 line.

delete [breakpoints] [*bnums*...]
                 Delete the breakpoints or watchpoints of the numbers speci-
                 fied as arguments. If no argument is specified, delete all break-
                 points (GDB asks confirmation, unless you have set confirm
                 off). You can abbreviate this command as d.

## 5.1.5 Disabling Breakpoints

Rather than deleting a breakpoint or watchpoint, you might prefer to
*disable* it. This makes the breakpoint inoperative as if it had been deleted,
but remembers the information on the breakpoint so that you can *enable* it
again later.

You disable and enable breakpoints and watchpoints with the enable and
disable commands, optionally specifying one or more breakpoint numbers
as arguments. Use info break or info watch to print a list of breakpoints
or watchpoints if you do not know which numbers to use.

A breakpoint or watchpoint can have any of four different states of en-
ablement:

- Enabled. The breakpoint will stop your program. A breakpoint set
  with the break command starts out in this state.

- Disabled. The breakpoint has no effect on your program.

- Enabled once. The breakpoint will stop your program, but when it does
  so it will become disabled. A breakpoint set with the tbreak command
  starts out in this state.

- Enabled for deletion. The breakpoint will stop your program, but immediately after it does so it will be deleted permanently.

You can use the following commands to enable or disable breakpoints and
watchpoints:

`disable` [`breakpoints`] [*bnums*...]

> Disable the specified breakpoints—or all breakpoints, if none are listed. A disabled breakpoint has no effect but is not forgotten. All options such as ignore-counts, conditions and commands are remembered in case the breakpoint is enabled again later. You may abbreviate `disable` as `dis`.

`enable` [`breakpoints`] [*bnums*...]

> Enable the specified breakpoints (or all defined breakpoints). They become effective once again in stopping your program.

`enable` [`breakpoints`] `once` *bnums*...

> Enable the specified breakpoints temporarily. Each will be disabled again the next time it stops your program.

`enable` [`breakpoints`] `delete` *bnums*...

> Enable the specified breakpoints to work once and then die. Each of the breakpoints will be deleted the next time it stops your program.

Save for a breakpoint set with `tbreak` (see Section 5.1.1 [Setting Breakpoints], page 30), breakpoints that you set are initially enabled; subsequently, they become disabled or enabled only when you use one of the commands above. (The command `until` can set and delete a breakpoint of its own, but it will not change the state of your other breakpoints; see Section 5.2 [Continuing and Stepping], page 40.)

## 5.1.6  Break Conditions

The simplest sort of breakpoint breaks every time your program reaches a specified place. You can also specify a *condition* for a breakpoint. A condition is just a Boolean expression in your programming language (see Section 8.1 [Expressions], page 57). A breakpoint with a condition evaluates the expression each time your program reaches it, and your program stops only if the condition is *true*.

This is the converse of using assertions for program validation; in that situation, you want to stop when the assertion is violated—that is, when the condition is false. In C, if you want to test an assertion expressed by the condition *assert*, you should set the condition '! *assert*' on the appropriate breakpoint.

Conditions are also accepted for watchpoints; you may not need them, since a watchpoint is inspecting the value of an expression anyhow—but it might be simpler, say, to just set a watchpoint on a variable name, and specify a condition that tests whether the new value is an interesting one.

Break conditions can have side effects, and may even call functions in
your program. This can be useful, for example, to activate functions that log
program progress, or to use your own print functions to format special data
structures. The effects are completely predictable unless there is another
enabled breakpoint at the same address. (In that case, GDB might see the
other breakpoint first and stop your program without checking the condition
of this one.) Note that breakpoint commands are usually more convenient
and flexible for the purpose of performing side effects when a breakpoint is
reached (see Section 5.1.7 [Breakpoint Command Lists], page 37).

Break conditions can be specified when a breakpoint is set, by using
'if' in the arguments to the `break` command. See Section 5.1.1 [Setting
Breakpoints], page 30. They can also be changed at any time with the
`condition` command. The `watch` command does not recognize the `if` keyword; `condition` is the only way to impose a further condition on a watchpoint.

condition *bnum expression*

>    Specify *expression* as the break condition for breakpoint or
>    watchpoint number *bnum*.   From now on, this breakpoint
>    will stop your program only if the value of *expression* is true
>    (nonzero, in C). When you use `condition`, GDB checks *ex-
>    pression* immediately for syntactic correctness, and to determine
>    whether symbols in it have referents in the context of your break-
>    point. GDB does not actually evaluate *expression* at the time
>    the `condition` command is given, however. See Section 8.1 [Ex-
>    pressions], page 57.

condition *bnum*

>    Remove the condition from breakpoint number *bnum*. It be-
>    comes an ordinary unconditional breakpoint.

A special case of a breakpoint condition is to stop only when the breakpoint has been reached a certain number of times. This is so useful that there
is a special way to do it, using the *ignore count* of the breakpoint. Every
breakpoint has an ignore count, which is an integer. Most of the time, the
ignore count is zero, and therefore has no effect. But if your program reaches
a breakpoint whose ignore count is positive, then instead of stopping, it just
decrements the ignore count by one and continues. As a result, if the ignore
count value is *n*, the breakpoint will not stop the next *n* times it is reached.

ignore *bnum count*

>    Set the ignore count of breakpoint number *bnum* to *count*. The
>    next *count* times the breakpoint is reached, your program's ex-
>    ecution will not stop; other than to decrement the ignore count,

GDB takes no action.

To make the breakpoint stop the next time it is reached, specify a count of zero.

**continue** *count*
**c** *count*
**fg** *count*    Continue execution of your program, setting the ignore count of the breakpoint where your program stopped to *count* minus one. Thus, your program will not stop at this breakpoint until the *count*'th time it is reached.

An argument to this command is meaningful only when your program stopped due to a breakpoint. At other times, the argument to **continue** is ignored.

The synonym **fg** is provided purely for convenience, and has exactly the same behavior as other forms of the command.

If a breakpoint has a positive ignore count and a condition, the condition is not checked. Once the ignore count reaches zero, the condition will be checked.

You could achieve the effect of the ignore count with a condition such as '**$foo-- <= 0**' using a debugger convenience variable that is decremented each time. See Section 8.9 [Convenience Variables], page 69.

### 5.1.7 Breakpoint Command Lists

You can give any breakpoint (or watchpoint) a series of commands to execute when your program stops due to that breakpoint. For example, you might want to print the values of certain expressions, or enable other breakpoints.

**commands** [*bnum*]
... *command-list* ...
**end**    Specify a list of commands for breakpoint number *bnum*. The commands themselves appear on the following lines. Type a line containing just **end** to terminate the commands.

To remove all commands from a breakpoint, type **commands** and follow it immediately with **end**; that is, give no commands.

With no *bnum* argument, **commands** refers to the last breakpoint or watchpoint set (not to the breakpoint most recently encountered).

Pressing **RET** as a means of repeating the last GDB command is disabled within a *command-list*.

You can use breakpoint commands to start your program up again. Simply use the `continue` command, or `step`, or any other command that resumes execution. Subsequent commands in the command list are ignored.

If the first command specified is `silent`, the usual message about stopping at a breakpoint is not printed. This may be desirable for breakpoints that are to print a specific message and then continue. If none of the remaining commands print anything, you will see no sign that the breakpoint was reached. `silent` is meaningful only at the beginning of a breakpoint command list.

The commands `echo` and `output` that allow you to print precisely controlled output are often useful in silent breakpoints. See Section 15.3 [Commands for Controlled Output], page 120.

For example, here is how you could use breakpoint commands to print the value of x at entry to `foo` whenever x is positive.

```
break foo if x>0
commands
silent
echo x is\040
output x
echo \n
cont
end
```

One application for breakpoint commands is to compensate for one bug so you can test for another. Put a breakpoint just after the erroneous line of code, give it a condition to detect the case in which something erroneous has been done, and give it commands to assign correct values to any variables that need them. End with the `continue` command so that your program does not stop, and start with the `silent` command so that no output is produced. Here is an example:

```
break 403
commands
silent
set x = y + 4
cont
end
```

One deficiency in the operation of automatically continuing breakpoints under Unix appears when your program uses raw mode for the terminal. GDB switches back to its own terminal modes (not raw) before executing commands, and then must switch back to raw mode when your program is continued. This causes any pending terminal input to be lost.

Under Unix, you can get around this problem by writing actions into the breakpoint condition rather than in commands. For example,

```
condition 5  (x = y + 4), 0
```

specifies a condition expression (see Section 8.1 [Expressions], page 57) that will change x as needed, then always have the value zero so your program will not stop. No input is lost here, because GDB evaluates break conditions without changing the terminal modes. When you want to have nontrivial conditions for performing the side effects, the operators '&&', '||' and '?...:' may be useful.

### 5.1.8 Breakpoint Menus

Some programming languages (notably C++) permit a single function name to be defined several times, for application in different contexts. This is called *overloading*. When a function name is overloaded, 'break *function*' is not enough to tell GDB where you want a breakpoint. GDB offers you a menu of numbered choices for different possible breakpoints, and waits for your selection with the prompt '>'. The first two options are always '[0] cancel' and '[1] all'. Typing 1 sets a breakpoint at each definition of *function*, and typing 0 aborts the **break** command without setting any new breakpoints.

For example, the following session excerpt shows an attempt to set a breakpoint at the overloaded symbol String::after. We choose three particular definitions of that function name:

```
(gdb) b String::after
[0] cancel
[1] all
[2] file:String.cc; line number:867
[3] file:String.cc; line number:860
[4] file:String.cc; line number:875
[5] file:String.cc; line number:853
[6] file:String.cc; line number:846
[7] file:String.cc; line number:735
> 2 4 6
Breakpoint 1 at 0xb26c: file String.cc, line 867.
Breakpoint 2 at 0xb344: file String.cc, line 875.
Breakpoint 3 at 0xafcc: file String.cc, line 846.
Multiple breakpoints were set.
Use the "delete" command to delete unwanted breakpoints.
(gdb)
```

### 5.1.9 "Cannot Insert Breakpoints"

Under some operating systems, breakpoints cannot be used in a program
if any other process is running that program. In this situation, attempting
to run or continue a program with a breakpoint causes GDB to stop the
other process.

When this happens, you have three ways to proceed:

1. Remove or disable the breakpoints, then continue.
2. Suspend GDB, and copy the file containing your program to a new name.
   Resume GDB and use the `exec-file` command to specify that GDB
   should run your program under that name. Then start your program
   again.
3. Relink your program so that the text segment is nonsharable, using the
   linker option '`-N`'. The operating system limitation may not apply to
   nonsharable executables.

## 5.2  Continuing and Stepping

*Continuing* means resuming program execution until your program com-
pletes normally. In contrast, *stepping* means executing just one more "step"
of your program, where "step" may mean either one line of source code,
or one machine instruction (depending on what particular command you
use). Either when continuing or when stepping, your program may stop
even sooner, due to a breakpoint or to a signal. (If due to a signal, you may
want to use `handle`, or use '`signal 0`' to resume execution. See Section 5.3
[Signals], page 43.)

continue [*ignore-count*]

> Resume program execution, at the address where your program
> last stopped; any breakpoints set at that address are bypassed.
> The optional argument *ignore-count* allows you to specify a fur-
> ther number of times to ignore a breakpoint at this location; its
> effect is like that of `ignore` (see Section 5.1.6 [Break Conditions],
> page 35).
>
> To resume execution at a different place, you can use `return` (see
> Section 11.4 [Returning from a Function], page 95) to go back
> to the calling function; or `jump` (see Section 11.2 [Continuing at
> a Different Address], page 94) to go to an arbitrary location in
> your program.

A typical technique for using stepping is to set a breakpoint (see Section 5.1 [Breakpoints Watchpoints and Exceptions], page 29) at the begin-

ning of the function or the section of your program where a problem is believed to lie, run your program until it stops at that breakpoint, and then step through the suspect area, examining the variables that are interesting, until you see the problem happen.

step          Continue running your program until control reaches a different source line, then stop it and return control to GDB. This command is abbreviated **s**.

> *Warning:* If you use the **step** command while control is within a function that was compiled without debugging information, execution will proceed until control reaches another function.

step *count*

Continue running as in **step**, but do so *count* times. If a breakpoint is reached or a signal not related to stepping occurs before *count* steps, stepping stops right away.

next [*count*]

Continue to the next source line in the current (innermost) stack frame. Similar to **step**, but any function calls appearing within the line of code are executed without stopping. Execution stops when control reaches a different line of code at the stack level which was executing when the **next** command was given. This command is abbreviated n.

An argument *count* is a repeat count, as for **step**.

**next** within a function that lacks debugging information acts like **step**, but any function calls appearing within the code of the function are executed without stopping.

finish        Continue running until just after function in the selected stack frame returns. Print the returned value (if any).

Contrast this with the **return** command (see Section 11.4 [Returning from a Function], page 95).

until

u             Continue running until a source line past the current line, in the current stack frame, is reached. This command is used to avoid single stepping through a loop more than once. It is like the **next** command, except that when **until** encounters a jump, it automatically continues execution until the program counter is greater than the address of the jump.

This means that when you reach the end of a loop after single stepping though it, **until** will cause your program to continue execution until the loop is exited. In contrast, a **next** command at the end of a loop will simply step back to the beginning of the loop, which would force you to step through the next iteration.

**until** always stops your program if it attempts to exit the current stack frame.

**until** may produce somewhat counterintuitive results if the order of machine code does not match the order of the source lines. For example, in the following excerpt from a debugging session, the **f** (**frame**) command shows that execution is stopped at line 206; yet when we use **until**, we get to line 195:

```
(gdb) f
#0  main (argc=4, argv=0xf7fffae8) at m4.c:206
206                   expand_input();
(gdb) until
195                   for ( ; argc > 0; NEXTARG) {
```

This happened because, for execution efficiency, the compiler had generated code for the loop closure test at the end, rather than the start, of the loop—even though the test in a C for-loop is written before the body of the loop. The **until** command appeared to step back to the beginning of the loop when it advanced to this expression; however, it has not really gone to an earlier statement—not in terms of the actual machine code.

**until** with no argument works by means of single instruction stepping, and hence is slower than **until** with an argument.

**until** *location*

**u** *location*   Continue running your program until either the specified location is reached, or the current stack frame returns. *location* is any of the forms of argument acceptable to **break** (see Section 5.1.1 [Setting Breakpoints], page 30). This form of the command uses breakpoints, and hence is quicker than **until** without an argument.

**stepi**

**si**            Execute one machine instruction, then stop and return to the debugger.

It is often useful to do '**display/i $pc**' when stepping by machine instructions. This will cause the next instruction to be executed to be displayed automatically at each stop. See Section 8.6 [Automatic Display], page 63.

An argument is a repeat count, as in **step**.

**nexti**

ni           Execute one machine instruction, but if it is a function call, proceed until the function returns.

An argument is a repeat count, as in `next`.

## 5.3 Signals

A signal is an asynchronous event that can happen in a program. The operating system defines the possible kinds of signals, and gives each kind a name and a number. For example, in Unix `SIGINT` is the signal a program gets when you type an interrupt (often `C-c`); `SIGSEGV` is the signal a program gets from referencing a place in memory far away from all the areas in use; `SIGALRM` occurs when the alarm clock timer goes off (which happens only if your program has requested an alarm).

Some signals, including `SIGALRM`, are a normal part of the functioning of your program. Others, such as `SIGSEGV`, indicate errors; these signals are *fatal* (kill your program immediately) if the program has not specified in advance some other way to handle the signal. `SIGINT` does not indicate an error in your program, but it is normally fatal so it can carry out the purpose of the interrupt: to kill the program.

GDB has the ability to detect any occurrence of a signal in your program. You can tell GDB in advance what to do for each kind of signal.

Normally, GDB is set up to ignore non-erroneous signals like `SIGALRM` (so as not to interfere with their role in the functioning of your program) but to stop your program immediately whenever an error signal happens. You can change these settings with the `handle` command.

`info signals`

Print a table of all the kinds of signals and how GDB has been told to handle each one. You can use this to see the signal numbers of all the defined types of signals.

`handle` *signal keywords*...

Change the way GDB handles signal *signal*. *signal* can be the number of a signal or its name (with or without the 'SIG' at the beginning). The *keywords* say what change to make.

The keywords allowed by the `handle` command can be abbreviated. Their full names are:

`nostop`    GDB should not stop your program when this signal happens. It may still print a message telling you that the signal has come in.

stop        GDB should stop your program when this signal happens. This implies the `print` keyword as well.

print      GDB should print a message when this signal happens.

noprint   GDB should not mention the occurrence of the signal at all. This implies the `nostop` keyword as well.

pass        GDB should allow your program to see this signal; your program will be able to handle the signal, or may be terminated if the signal is fatal and not handled.

nopass    GDB should not allow your program to see this signal.

When a signal has been set to stop your program, it cannot see the signal until you continue. It will see the signal then, if `pass` is in effect for the signal in question *at that time*. In other words, after GDB reports a signal, you can use the `handle` command with `pass` or `nopass` to control whether that signal will be seen by your program when you later continue it.

You can also use the `signal` command to prevent your program from seeing a signal, or cause it to see a signal it normally would not see, or to give it any signal at any time. For example, if your program stopped due to some sort of memory reference error, you might store correct values into the erroneous variables and continue, hoping to see more execution; but your program would probably terminate immediately as a result of the fatal signal once it saw the signal. To prevent this, you can continue with '`signal 0`'. See Section 11.3 [Giving your Program a Signal], page 95.

# 6 Examining the Stack

When your program has stopped, the first thing you need to know is where it stopped and how it got there.

Each time your program performs a function call, the information about where in your program the call was made from is saved in a block of data called a *stack frame*. The frame also contains the arguments of the call and the local variables of the function that was called. All the stack frames are allocated in a region of memory called the *call stack*.

When your program stops, the GDB commands for examining the stack allow you to see all of this information.

One of the stack frames is *selected* by GDB and many GDB commands refer implicitly to the selected frame. In particular, whenever you ask GDB for the value of a variable in your program, the value is found in the selected frame. There are special GDB commands to select whichever frame you are interested in.

When your program stops, GDB automatically selects the currently executing frame and describes it briefly as the `frame` command does (see Section 6.4 [Information About a Frame], page 48).

## 6.1 Stack Frames

The call stack is divided up into contiguous pieces called *stack frames*, or *frames* for short; each frame is the data associated with one call to one function. The frame contains the arguments given to the function, the function's local variables, and the address at which the function is executing.

When your program is started, the stack has only one frame, that of the function `main`. This is called the *initial* frame or the *outermost* frame. Each time a function is called, a new frame is made. Each time a function returns, the frame for that function invocation is eliminated. If a function is recursive, there can be many frames for the same function. The frame for the function in which execution is actually occurring is called the *innermost* frame. This is the most recently created of all the stack frames that still exist.

Inside your program, stack frames are identified by their addresses. A stack frame consists of many bytes, each of which has its own address; each kind of computer has a convention for choosing one of those bytes whose address serves as the address of the frame. Usually this address is kept in a register called the *frame pointer register* while execution is going on in that frame.

GDB assigns numbers to all existing stack frames, starting with zero for the innermost frame, one for the frame that called it, and so on upward. These numbers do not really exist in your program; they are assigned by GDB to give you a way of designating stack frames in GDB commands.

Some compilers allow functions to be compiled so that they operate without stack frames. (For example, the `gcc` option '`-fomit-frame-pointer`' will generate functions without a frame.) This is occasionally done with heavily used library functions to save the frame setup time. GDB has limited facilities for dealing with these function invocations. If the innermost function invocation has no stack frame, GDB will nevertheless regard it as though it had a separate frame, which is numbered zero as usual, allowing correct tracing of the function call chain. However, GDB has no provision for frameless functions elsewhere in the stack.

## 6.2 Backtraces

A backtrace is a summary of how your program got where it is. It shows one line per frame, for many frames, starting with the currently executing frame (frame zero), followed by its caller (frame one), and on up the stack.

`backtrace`
`bt`                 Print a backtrace of the entire stack: one line per frame for all frames in the stack.

You can stop the backtrace at any time by typing the system interrupt character, normally `C-c`.

`backtrace` *n*
`bt` *n*             Similar, but print only the innermost *n* frames.

`backtrace` *-n*
`bt` *-n*            Similar, but print only the outermost *n* frames.

The names `where` and `info stack` (abbreviated `info s`) are additional aliases for `backtrace`.

Each line in the backtrace shows the frame number and the function name. The program counter value is also shown—unless you use `set print address off`. The backtrace also shows the source file name and line number, as well as the arguments to the function. The program counter value is omitted if it is at the beginning of the code for that line number.

Here is an example of a backtrace. It was made with the command '`bt 3`', so it shows the innermost three frames.

```
#0  m4_traceon (obs=0x24eb0, argc=1, argv=0x2b8c8)
    at builtin.c:993
#1  0x6e38 in expand_macro (sym=0x2b600) at macro.c:242
#2  0x6840 in expand_token (obs=0x0, t=177664, td=0xf7fffb08)
    at macro.c:71
(More stack frames follow...)
```

The display for frame zero does not begin with a program counter value, indicating that your program has stopped at the beginning of the code for line 993 of `builtin.c`.

## 6.3  Selecting a Frame

Most commands for examining the stack and other data in your program work on whichever stack frame is selected at the moment. Here are the commands for selecting a stack frame; all of them finish by printing a brief description of the stack frame just selected.

**frame** *n*
**f** *n*          Select frame number *n*. Recall that frame zero is the innermost (currently executing) frame, frame one is the frame that called the innermost one, and so on. The highest-numbered frame is **main**'s frame.

**frame** *addr*
**f** *addr*       Select the frame at address *addr*. This is useful mainly if the chaining of stack frames has been damaged by a bug, making it impossible for GDB to assign numbers properly to all frames. In addition, this can be useful when your program has multiple stacks and switches between them.

On the SPARC architecture, **frame** needs two addresses to select an arbitrary frame: a frame pointer and a stack pointer.

**up** *n*         Move *n* frames up the stack. For positive numbers *n*, this advances toward the outermost frame, to higher frame numbers, to frames that have existed longer. *n* defaults to one.

**down** *n*       Move *n* frames down the stack. For positive numbers *n*, this advances toward the innermost frame, to lower frame numbers, to frames that were created more recently. *n* defaults to one. You may abbreviate **down** as **do**.

All of these commands end by printing two lines of output describing the frame. The first line shows the frame number, the function name, the arguments, and the source file and line number of execution in that frame. The second line shows the text of that source line.

For example:

```
(gdb) up
#1  0x22f0 in main (argc=1, argv=0xf7fffbf4, env=0xf7fffbfc)
    at env.c:10
10                read_input_file (argv[i]);
```

After such a printout, the `list` command with no arguments will print ten lines centered on the point of execution in the frame. See Section 7.1 [Printing Source Lines], page 51.

up-silently *n*
down-silently *n*

> These two commands are variants of `up` and `down`, respectively; they differ in that they do their work silently, without causing display of the new frame. They are intended primarily for use in GDB command scripts, where the output might be unnecessary and distracting.

## 6.4 Information About a Frame

There are several other commands to print information about the selected stack frame.

frame
f

> When used without any argument, this command does not change which frame is selected, but prints a brief description of the currently selected stack frame. It can be abbreviated `f`. With an argument, this command is used to select a stack frame. See Section 6.3 [Selecting a Frame], page 47.

info frame
info f

> This command prints a verbose description of the selected stack frame, including the address of the frame, the addresses of the next frame down (called by this frame) and the next frame up (caller of this frame), the language that the source code corresponding to this frame was written in, the address of the frame's arguments, the program counter saved in it (the address of execution in the caller frame), and which registers were saved in the frame. The verbose description is useful when something has gone wrong that has made the stack format fail to fit the usual conventions.

info frame *addr*
info f *addr*

> Print a verbose description of the frame at address *addr*, without selecting that frame. The selected frame remains unchanged by this command.

`info args`   Print the arguments of the selected frame, each on a separate line.

`info locals`

> Print the local variables of the selected frame, each on a separate line. These are all variables (declared either static or automatic) accessible at the point of execution of the selected frame.

`info catch`

> Print a list of all the exception handlers that are active in the current stack frame at the current point of execution. To see other exception handlers, visit the associated frame (using the `up`, `down`, or `frame` commands); then type `info catch`. See Section 5.1.3 [Breakpoints and Exceptions], page 32.

# 7  Examining Source Files

GDB can print parts of your program's source, since the debugging information recorded in the program tells GDB what source files were used
to build it. When your program stops, GDB spontaneously prints the line
where it stopped. Likewise, when you select a stack frame (see Section 6.3
[Selecting a Frame], page 47), GDB prints the line where execution in that
frame has stopped. You can print other portions of source files by explicit
command.

If you use GDB through its GNU Emacs interface, you may prefer to
use Emacs facilities to view source; see Chapter 16 [Using GDB under GNU
Emacs], page 123.

## 7.1  Printing Source Lines

To print lines from a source file, use the `list` command (abbreviated `l`).
There are several ways to specify what part of the file you want to print.

Here are the forms of the `list` command most commonly used:

`list` *linenum*

>   Print lines centered around line number *linenum* in the current
>   source file.

`list` *function*

>   Print lines centered around the beginning of function *function*.

`list`

>   Print more lines. If the last lines printed were printed with a
>   `list` command, this prints lines following the last lines printed;
>   however, if the last line printed was a solitary line printed as
>   part of displaying a stack frame (see Chapter 6 [Examining the
>   Stack], page 45), this prints lines centered around that line.

`list -`

>   Print lines just before the lines last printed.

By default, GDB prints ten source lines with any of these forms of the
`list` command. You can change this using `set listsize`:

`set listsize` *count*

>   Make the `list` command display *count* source lines (unless the
>   `list` argument explicitly specifies some other number).

`show listsize`

>   Display the number of lines that `list` will currently display by
>   default.

Repeating a `list` command with RET discards the argument, so it is equivalent to typing just `list`. This is more useful than listing the same lines again. An exception is made for an argument of '-'; that argument is preserved in repetition so that each repetition moves up in the source file.

In general, the `list` command expects you to supply zero, one or two *linespecs*. Linespecs specify source lines; there are several ways of writing them but the effect is always to specify some source line. Here is a complete description of the possible arguments for `list`:

`list` *linespec*

> Print lines centered around the line specified by *linespec*.

`list` *first,last*

> Print lines from *first* to *last*. Both arguments are linespecs.

`list ,`*last*     Print lines ending with *last*.

`list` *first,*

> Print lines starting with *first*.

`list +`     Print lines just after the lines last printed.

`list -`     Print lines just before the lines last printed.

`list`       As described in the preceding table.

Here are the ways of specifying a single source line—all the kinds of linespec.

*number*     Specifies line *number* of the current source file. When a `list` command has two linespecs, this refers to the same source file as the first linespec.

*+offset*    Specifies the line *offset* lines after the last line printed. When used as the second linespec in a `list` command that has two, this specifies the line *offset* lines down from the first linespec.

*-offset*    Specifies the line *offset* lines before the last line printed.

*filename:number*

> Specifies line *number* in the source file *filename*.

*function*   Specifies the line of the open-brace that begins the body of the function *function*.

*filename:function*

> Specifies the line of the open-brace that begins the body of the function *function* in the file *filename*. You only need the file name with a function name to avoid ambiguity when there are identically named functions in different source files.

*\*address*  Specifies the line containing the program address *address*. *address* may be any expression.

## 7.2 Searching Source Files

There are two commands for searching through the current source file for a regular expression.

**forward-search** *regexp*
**search** *regexp*

> The command '**forward-search** *regexp*' checks each line, starting with the one following the last line listed, for a match for *regexp*. It lists the line that is found. You can use synonym '**search** *regexp*' or abbreviate the command name as **fo**.

**reverse-search** *regexp*

> The command '**reverse-search** *regexp*' checks each line, starting with the one before the last line listed and going backward, for a match for *regexp*. It lists the line that is found. You can abbreviate this command as **rev**.

## 7.3 Specifying Source Directories

Executable programs sometimes do not record the directories of the source files from which they were compiled, just the names. Even when they do, the directories could be moved between the compilation and your debugging session. GDB has a list of directories to search for source files; this is called the *source path*. Each time GDB wants a source file, it tries all the directories in the list, in the order they are present in the list, until it finds a file with the desired name. Note that the executable search path is *not* used for this purpose. Neither is the current working directory, unless it happens to be in the source path.

If GDB cannot find a source file in the source path, and the object program records a directory, GDB tries that directory too. If the source path is empty, and there is no record of the compilation directory, GDB will, as a last resort, look in the current directory.

Whenever you reset or rearrange the source path, GDB will clear out any information it has cached about where source files are found, where each line is in the file, etc.

When you start GDB, its source path is empty. To add other directories, use the **directory** command.

**directory** *dirname* ...

> Add directory *dirname* to the front of the source path. Several directory names may be given to this command, separated by

':' or whitespace. You may specify a directory that is already in the source path; this moves it forward, so it will be searched sooner.

You can use the string '$cdir' to refer to the compilation directory (if one is recorded), and '$cwd' to refer to the current working directory. '$cwd' is not the same as '.'—the former tracks the current working directory as it changes during your GDB session, while the latter is immediately expanded to the current directory at the time you add an entry to the source path.

**directory**

Reset the source path to empty again. This requires confirmation.

**show directories**

Print the source path: show which directories it contains.

If your source path is cluttered with directories that are no longer of interest, GDB may sometimes cause confusion by finding the wrong versions of source. You can correct the situation as follows:

1. Use **directory** with no argument to reset the source path to empty.
2. Use **directory** with suitable arguments to reinstall the directories you want in the source path. You can add all the directories in one command.

## 7.4  Source and Machine Code

You can use the command **info line** to map source lines to program addresses (and vice versa), and the command **disassemble** to display a range of addresses as machine instructions.

**info line** *linespec*

Print the starting and ending addresses of the compiled code for source line *linespec*. You can specify source lines in any of the ways understood by the **list** command (see Section 7.1 [Printing Source Lines], page 51).

For example, we can use **info line** to discover the location of the object code for the first line of function m4_changequote:

```
(gdb) info line m4_changecom
Line 895 of "builtin.c" starts at pc 0x634c and ends at 0x6350.
```

We can also inquire (using *addr* as the form for *linespec*) what source line covers a particular address:

```
(gdb) info line *0x63ff
Line 926 of "builtin.c" starts at pc 0x63e4 and ends at 0x6404.
```

After `info line`, the default address for the `x` command is changed to the starting address of the line, so that '`x/i`' is sufficient to begin examining the machine code (see Section 8.5 [Examining Memory], page 61). Also, this address is saved as the value of the convenience variable `$_` (see Section 8.9 [Convenience Variables], page 69).

`disassemble`

> This specialized command is provided to dump a range of memory as machine instructions. The default memory range is the function surrounding the program counter of the selected frame. A single argument to this command is a program counter value; the function surrounding this value will be dumped. Two arguments (separated by one or more spaces) specify a range of addresses (first inclusive, second exclusive) to be dumped.

We can use `disassemble` to inspect the object code range shown in the last `info line` example:

```
(gdb) disas 0x63e4 0x6404
Dump of assembler code from 0x63e4 to 0x6404:
0x63e4 builtin_init+5340:    ble 0x63f8 builtin_init+5360
0x63e8 builtin_init+5344:    sethi %hi(0x4c00), %o0
0x63ec builtin_init+5348:    ld [%i1+4], %o0
0x63f0 builtin_init+5352:    b 0x63fc builtin_init+5364
0x63f4 builtin_init+5356:    ld [%o0+4], %o0
0x63f8 builtin_init+5360:    or %o0, 0x1a4, %o0
0x63fc builtin_init+5364:    call 0x9288 path_search
0x6400 builtin_init+5368:    nop
End of assembler dump.
(gdb)
```

# 8  Examining Data

The usual way to examine data in your program is with the `print` command (abbreviated `p`), or its synonym `inspect`. It evaluates and prints the value of an expression of the language your program is written in (see Chapter 9 [Using GDB with Different Languages], page 73).

`print` *exp*
`print /f` *exp*

> *exp* is an expression (in the source language). By default the value of *exp* is printed in a format appropriate to its data type; you can choose a different format by specifying '`/f`', where *f* is a letter specifying the format; see Section 8.4 [Output Formats], page 60.

`print`
`print /f`   If you omit *exp*, GDB displays the last value again (from the *value history*; see Section 8.8 [Value History], page 68). This allows you to conveniently inspect the same value in an alternative format.

A more low-level way of examining data is with the `x` command. It examines data in memory at a specified address and prints it in a specified format. See Section 8.5 [Examining Memory], page 61.

If you are interested in information about types, or about how the fields of a struct or class are declared, use the `ptype` *exp* command rather than `print`. See Chapter 10 [Examining the Symbol Table], page 89.

## 8.1  Expressions

`print` and many other GDB commands accept an expression and compute its value. Any kind of constant, variable or operator defined by the programming language you are using is legal in an expression in GDB. This includes conditional expressions, function calls, casts and string constants. It unfortunately does not include symbols defined by preprocessor `#define` commands.

Because C is so widespread, most of the expressions shown in examples in this manual are in C. See Chapter 9 [Using GDB with Different Languages], page 73, for information on how to use expressions in other languages.

In this section, we discuss operators that you can use in GDB expressions regardless of your programming language.

Casts are supported in all languages, not just in C, because it is so useful to cast a number into a pointer so as to examine a structure at that address in memory.

GDB supports these operators in addition to those of programming languages:

@           '@' is a binary operator for treating parts of memory as arrays. See Section 8.3 [Artificial Arrays], page 59, for more information.

::          '::' allows you to specify a variable in terms of the file or function where it is defined. See Section 8.2 [Program Variables], page 58.

{*type*} *addr*

Refers to an object of type *type* stored at address *addr* in memory. *addr* may be any expression whose value is an integer or pointer (but parentheses are required around binary operators, just as in a cast). This construct is allowed regardless of what kind of data is normally supposed to reside at *addr*.

## 8.2 Program Variables

The most common kind of expression to use is the name of a variable in your program.

Variables in expressions are understood in the selected stack frame (see Section 6.3 [Selecting a Frame], page 47); they must either be global (or static) or be visible according to the scope rules of the programming language from the point of execution in that frame. This means that in the function

```
foo (a)
     int a;
{
  bar (a);
  {
    int b = test ();
    bar (b);
  }
}
```

the variable a is usable whenever your program is executing within the function foo, but the variable b is visible only while your program is executing inside the block in which b is declared.

There is an exception: you can refer to a variable or function whose scope is a single source file even if the current execution point is not in this file. But it is possible to have more than one such variable or function with the same name (in different source files). If that happens, referring to that name has unpredictable effects. If you wish, you can specify a variable in a particular file, using the colon-colon notation:

    file::variable

Here *file* is the name of the source file whose variable you want.

This use of ':: ' is very rarely in conflict with the very similar use of the same notation in C++. GDB also supports use of the C++ scope resolution operator in GDB expressions.

> *Warning:* Occasionally, a local variable may appear to have the wrong value at certain points in a function—just after entry to the function, and just before exit. You may see this problem when you are stepping by machine instructions. This is because on most machines, it takes more than one instruction to set up a stack frame (including local variable definitions); if you are stepping by machine instructions, variables may appear to have the wrong values until the stack frame is completely built. On function exit, it usually also takes more than one machine instruction to destroy a stack frame; after you begin stepping through that group of instructions, local variable definitions may be gone.

## 8.3  Artificial Arrays

It is often useful to print out several successive objects of the same type in memory; a section of an array, or an array of dynamically determined size for which only a pointer exists in the program.

This can be done by constructing an *artificial array* with the binary operator '@'. The left operand of '@' should be the first element of the desired array, as an individual object. The right operand should be the desired length of the array. The result is an array value whose elements are all of the type of the left argument. The first element is actually the left argument; the second element comes from bytes of memory immediately following those that hold the first element, and so on. Here is an example. If a program says

    int *array = (int *) malloc (len * sizeof (int));

you can print the contents of array with

    p *array@len

The left operand of '@' must reside in memory. Array values made with '@' in this way behave just like other arrays in terms of subscripting, and are coerced to pointers when used in expressions. Artificial arrays most often appear in expressions via the value history (see Section 8.8 [Value History], page 68), after printing one out.)

Sometimes the artificial array mechanism is not quite enough; in moderately complex data structures, the elements of interest may not actually be adjacent—for example, if you are interested in the values of pointers in an array. One useful work-around in this situation is to use a convenience variable (see Section 8.9 [Convenience Variables], page 69) as a counter in an expression that prints the first interesting value, and then repeat that expression via RET. For instance, suppose you have an array dtab of pointers to structures, and you are interested in the values of a field fv in each structure. Here is an example of what you might type:

```
set $i = 0
p dtab[$i++]->fv
RET
RET
...
```

## 8.4 Output Formats

By default, GDB prints a value according to its data type. Sometimes this is not what you want. For example, you might want to print a number in hex, or a pointer in decimal. Or you might want to view data in memory at a certain address as a character string or as an instruction. To do these things, specify an *output format* when you print a value.

The simplest use of output formats is to say how to print a value already computed. This is done by starting the arguments of the print command with a slash and a format letter. The format letters supported are:

x        Regard the bits of the value as an integer, and print the integer in hexadecimal.

d        Print as integer in signed decimal.

u        Print as integer in unsigned decimal.

o        Print as integer in octal.

t        Print as integer in binary. The letter 't' stands for "two".

a        Print as an address, both absolute in hex and as an offset from the nearest preceding symbol. This format can be used to discover where (in what function) an unknown address is located:

```
(gdb) p/a 0x54320
$3 = 0x54320 <_initialize_vx+396>
```

c        Regard as an integer and print it as a character constant.

f            Regard the bits of the value as a floating point number and print using typical floating point syntax.

For example, to print the program counter in hex (see Section 8.10 [Registers], page 70), type

```
p/x $pc
```

Note that no space is required before the slash; this is because command names in GDB cannot contain a slash.

To reprint the last value in the value history with a different format, you can use the `print` command with just a format and no expression. For example, '`p/x`' reprints the last value in hex.

## 8.5  Examining Memory

You can use the command x (for "examine") to examine memory in any of several formats, independently of your program's data types.

x/*nfu addr*
x *addr*
x            Use the x command to examine memory.

*n*, *f*, and *u* are all optional parameters that specify how much memory to display and how to format it; *addr* is an expression giving the address where you want to start displaying memory. If you use defaults for *nfu*, you need not type the slash '/'. Several commands set convenient defaults for *addr*.

*n*, the repeat count

The repeat count is a decimal integer; the default is 1. It specifies how much memory (counting by units *u*) to display.

*f*, the display format

The display format is one of the formats used by `print`, or '`s`' (null-terminated string) or '`i`' (machine instruction). The default is '`x`' (hexadecimal) initially, or the format from the last time you used either x or `print`.

*u*, the unit size

The unit size is any of

b            Bytes.

h            Halfwords (two bytes).

w            Words (four bytes). This is the initial default.

g            Giant words (eight bytes).

Each time you specify a unit size with x, that size becomes the default unit the next time you use x. (For the 's' and 'i' formats, the unit size is ignored and is normally not written.)

*addr*, starting display address

*addr* is the address where you want GDB to begin displaying memory. The expression need not have a pointer value (though it may); it is always interpreted as an integer address of a byte of memory. See Section 8.1 [Expressions], page 57, for more information on expressions. The default for *addr* is usually just after the last address examined—but several other commands also set the default address: info breakpoints (to the address of the last breakpoint listed), info line (to the starting address of a line), and print (if you use it to display a value from memory).

For example, 'x/3uh 0x54320' is a request to display three halfwords (h) of memory, formatted as unsigned decimal integers ('u'), starting at address 0x54320. 'x/4xw $sp' prints the four words ('w') of memory above the stack pointer (here, '$sp'; see Section 8.10 [Registers], page 70) in hexadecimal ('x').

Since the letters indicating unit sizes are all distinct from the letters specifying output formats, you do not have to remember whether unit size or format comes first; either order will work. The output specifications '4xw' and '4wx' mean exactly the same thing. (However, the count *n* must come first; 'wx4' will not work.)

Even though the unit size *u* is ignored for the formats 's' and 'i', you might still want to use a count *n*; for example, '3i' specifies that you want to see three machine instructions, including any operands. The command disassemble gives an alternative way of inspecting machine instructions; see Section 7.4 [Machine Code], page 54.

All the defaults for the arguments to x are designed to make it easy to continue scanning memory with minimal specifications each time you use x. For example, after you have inspected three machine instructions with 'x/3i addr', you can inspect the next seven with just 'x/7'. If you use RET to repeat the x command, the repeat count *n* is used again; the other arguments default as for successive uses of x.

The addresses and contents printed by the x command are not saved in the value history because there is often too much of them and they would get in the way. Instead, GDB makes these values available for subsequent use in expressions as values of the convenience variables $_ and $__. After an x command, the last address examined is available for use in expressions in the convenience variable $_. The contents of that address, as examined, are available in the convenience variable $_ _.

If the **x** command has a repeat count, the address and contents saved are from the last memory unit printed; this is not the same as the last address printed if several units were printed on the last line of output.

## 8.6 Automatic Display

If you find that you want to print the value of an expression frequently (to see how it changes), you might want to add it to the *automatic display list* so that GDB will print its value each time your program stops. Each expression added to the list is given a number to identify it; to remove an expression from the list, you specify that number. The automatic display looks like this:

```
2: foo = 38
3: bar[5] = (struct hack *) 0x3804
```

This shows item numbers, expressions and their current values. As with displays you request manually using **x** or **print**, you can specify the output format you prefer; in fact, **display** decides whether to use **print** or **x** depending on how elaborate your format specification is—it uses **x** if you specify a unit size, or one of the two formats ('i' and 's') that are only supported by **x**; otherwise it uses **print**.

**display** *exp*

> Add the expression *exp* to the list of expressions to display each time your program stops. See Section 8.1 [Expressions], page 57.
>
> **display** will not repeat if you press RET again after using it.

**display/**fmt *exp*

> For *fmt* specifying only a display format and not a size or count, add the expression *exp* to the auto-display list but arranges to display it each time in the specified format *fmt*. See Section 8.4 [Output Formats], page 60.

**display/**fmt *addr*

> For *fmt* 'i' or 's', or including a unit-size or a number of units, add the expression *addr* as a memory address to be examined each time your program stops. Examining means in effect doing 'x/fmt addr'. See Section 8.5 [Examining Memory], page 61.

For example, 'display/i $pc' can be helpful, to see the machine instruction about to be executed each time execution stops ('$pc' is a common name for the program counter; see Section 8.10 [Registers], page 70).

undisplay *dnums*...
delete display *dnums*...

>       Remove item numbers *dnums* from the list of expressions to
>       display.
>
>       undisplay will not repeat if you press RET after using it. (Oth-
>       erwise you would just get the error 'No display number ...'.)

disable display *dnums*...

>       Disable the display of item numbers *dnums*. A disabled display
>       item is not printed automatically, but is not forgotten. It may
>       be enabled again later.

enable display *dnums*...

>       Enable display of item numbers *dnums*. It becomes effective
>       once again in auto display of its expression, until you specify
>       otherwise.

display   Display the current values of the expressions on the list, just as
>         is done when your program stops.

info display

>       Print the list of expressions previously set up to display automat-
>       ically, each one with its item number, but without showing the
>       values. This includes disabled expressions, which are marked as
>       such. It also includes expressions which would not be displayed
>       right now because they refer to automatic variables not currently
>       available.

If a display expression refers to local variables, then it does not make
sense outside the lexical context for which it was set up. Such an expression
is disabled when execution enters a context where one of its variables is not
defined. For example, if you give the command display last_char while
inside a function with an argument last_char, then this argument will be
displayed while your program continues to stop inside that function. When it
stops elsewhere—where there is no variable last_char—display is disabled.
The next time your program stops where last_char is meaningful, you can
enable the display expression once again.

## 8.7  Print Settings

GDB provides the following ways to control how arrays, structures, and
symbols are printed.

These settings are useful for debugging programs in any language:

set print address

**set print address on**

> GDB will print memory addresses showing the location of stack traces, structure values, pointer values, breakpoints, and so forth, even when it also displays the contents of those addresses. The default is on. For example, this is what a stack frame display looks like, with **set print address on**:

```
(gdb) f
#0  set_quotes (lq=0x34c78 "<<", rq=0x34c88 ">>")
    at input.c:530
530          if (lquote != def_lquote)
```

**set print address off**

> Do not print addresses when displaying their contents. For example, this is the same stack frame displayed with **set print address off**:

```
(gdb) set print addr off
(gdb) f
#0  set_quotes (lq="<<", rq=">>") at input.c:530
530              if (lquote != def_lquote)
```

**show print address**

> Show whether or not addresses are to be printed.

**set print array**
**set print array on**

> GDB will pretty print arrays. This format is more convenient to read, but uses more space. The default is off.

**set print array off.**

> Return to compressed format for arrays.

**show print array**

> Show whether compressed or pretty format is selected for displaying arrays.

**set print elements** *number-of-elements*

> If GDB is printing a large array, it will stop printing after it has printed the number of elements set by the **set print elements** command. This limit also applies to the display of strings.

**show print elements**

> Display the number of elements of a large array that GDB will print before losing patience.

`set print pretty on`

> Cause GDB to print structures in an indented format with one
> member per line, like this:
>
> ```
> $1 = {
>   next = 0x0,
>   flags = {
>     sweet = 1,
>     sour = 1
>   },
>   meat = 0x54 "Pork"
> }
> ```

`set print pretty off`

> Cause GDB to print structures in a compact format, like this:
>
> ```
> $1 = {next = 0x0, flags = {sweet = 1, sour = 1}, meat \
> = 0x54 "Pork"}
> ```
>
> This is the default format.

`show print pretty`

> Show which format GDB will use to print structures.

`set print sevenbit-strings on`

> Print using only seven-bit characters; if this option is set, GDB
> will display any eight-bit characters (in strings or character val-
> ues) using the notation \nnn. For example, M-a is displayed as
> \341.

`set print sevenbit-strings off`

> Print using either seven-bit or eight-bit characters, as required.
> This is the default.

`show print sevenbit-strings`

> Show whether or not GDB will print only seven-bit characters.

`set print union on`

> Tell GDB to print unions which are contained in structures. This
> is the default setting.

`set print union off`

> Tell GDB not to print unions which are contained in structures.

`show print union`

> Ask GDB whether or not it will print unions which are contained
> in structures.
>
> For example, given the declarations

```
        typedef enum {Tree, Bug} Species;
        typedef enum {Big_tree, Acorn, Seedling} Tree_forms;
        typedef enum {Caterpillar, Cocoon, Butterfly}
                    Bug_forms;

        struct thing {
          Species it;
          union {
            Tree_forms tree;
            Bug_forms bug;
          } form;
        };
```

```
        struct thing foo = {Tree, {Acorn}};
```
with `set print union on` in effect 'p foo' would print

```
        $1 = {it = Tree, form = {tree = Acorn, bug = Cocoon}}
```
and with `set print union off` in effect it would print

```
        $1 = {it = Tree, form = {...}}
```
These settings are of interest when debugging C++ programs:

`set print demangle`
`set print demangle on`

Print C++ names in their source form rather than in the mangled form in which they are passed to the assembler and linker for type-safe linkage. The default is on.

`show print demangle`

Show whether C++ names will be printed in mangled or demangled form.

`set print asm-demangle`
`set print asm-demangle on`

Print C++ names in their source form rather than their mangled form, even in assembler code printouts such as instruction disassemblies. The default is off.

`show print asm-demangle`

Show whether C++ names in assembly listings will be printed in mangled or demangled form.

`set print object`
`set print object on`

When displaying a pointer to an object, identify the *actual* (derived) type of the object rather than the *declared* type, using the virtual function table.

`set print object off`

Display only the declared type of objects, without reference to the virtual function table. This is the default setting.

`show print object`

Show whether actual, or declared, object types will be displayed.

`set print vtbl`
`set print vtbl on`

Pretty print C++ virtual function tables. The default is off.

`set print vtbl off`

Do not pretty print C++ virtual function tables.

`show print vtbl`

Show whether C++ virtual function tables are pretty printed, or not.

## 8.8 Value History

Values printed by the `print` command are saved in GDB's *value history* so that you can refer to them in other expressions. Values are kept until the symbol table is re-read or discarded (for example with the `file` or `symbol-file` commands). When the symbol table changes, the value history is discarded, since the values may contain pointers back to the types defined in the symbol table.

The values printed are given *history numbers* for you to refer to them by. These are successive integers starting with one. `print` shows you the history number assigned to a value by printing '$*num* = ' before the value; here *num* is the history number.

To refer to any previous value, use '$' followed by the value's history number. The way `print` labels its output is designed to remind you of this. Just $ refers to the most recent value in the history, and $$ refers to the value before that. $$*n* refers to the *n*th value from the end; $$2 is the value just prior to $$, $$1 is equivalent to $$, and $$0 is equivalent to $.

For example, suppose you have just printed a pointer to a structure and want to see the contents of the structure. It suffices to type

    p *$

If you have a chain of structures where the component `next` points to the next one, you can print the contents of the next one with this:

```
p *$.next
```
You can print successive links in the chain by repeating this command—which you can do by just typing RET.

Note that the history records values, not expressions. If the value of x is 4 and you type these commands:

```
print x
set x=5
```
then the value recorded in the value history by the print command remains 4 even though the value of x has changed.

**show values**

> Print the last ten values in the value history, with their item numbers. This is like 'p $$9' repeated ten times, except that show values does not change the history.

**show values** *n*

> Print ten history values centered on history item number *n*.

**show values +**

> Print ten history values just after the values last printed. If no more values are available, produces no display.

Pressing RET to repeat show values *n* has exactly the same effect as 'show values +'.

## 8.9 Convenience Variables

GDB provides *convenience variables* that you can use within GDB to hold on to a value and refer to it later. These variables exist entirely within GDB; they are not part of your program, and setting a convenience variable has no direct effect on further execution of your program. That is why you can use them freely.

Convenience variables are prefixed with '$'. Any name preceded by '$' can be used for a convenience variable, unless it is one of the predefined machine-specific register names (see Section 8.10 [Registers], page 70). (Value history references, in contrast, are *numbers* preceded by '$'. See Section 8.8 [Value History], page 68.)

You can save a value in a convenience variable with an assignment expression, just as you would set a variable in your program. For example:

```
set $foo = *object_ptr
```
would save in $foo the value contained in the object pointed to by object_ptr.

Using a convenience variable for the first time creates it; but its value is **void** until you assign a new value. You can alter the value with another assignment at any time.

Convenience variables have no fixed types. You can assign a convenience variable any type of value, including structures and arrays, even if that variable already has a value of a different type. The convenience variable, when used as an expression, has the type of its current value.

**show convenience**

Print a list of convenience variables used so far, and their values. Abbreviated **show con**.

One of the ways to use a convenience variable is as a counter to be incremented or a pointer to be advanced. For example, to print a field from successive elements of an array of structures:

```
set $i = 0
print bar[$i++]->contents
```
... *repeat that command by typing* RET.

Some convenience variables are created automatically by GDB and given values likely to be useful.

**$_**
> The variable **$_** is automatically set by the **x** command to the last address examined (see Section 8.5 [Examining Memory], page 61). Other commands which provide a default address for **x** to examine also set **$_** to that address; these commands include **info line** and **info breakpoint**. The type of **$_** is **void \*** except when set by the **x** command, in which case it is a pointer to the type of **$__**.

**$__**
> The variable **$__** is automatically set by the **x** command to the value found in the last address examined. Its type is chosen to match the format in which the data was printed.

## 8.10 Registers

You can refer to machine register contents, in expressions, as variables with names starting with '**$**'. The names of registers are different for each machine; use **info registers** to see the names used on your machine.

**info registers**

> Print the names and values of all registers except floating-point registers (in the selected stack frame).

`info all-registers`

> Print the names and values of all registers, including floating-point registers.

`info registers regname`

> Print the relativized value of register *regname*. *regname* may be any register name valid on the machine you are using, with or without the initial '$'.

GDB has four "standard" register names that are available (in expressions) on most machines—whenever they do not conflict with an architecture's canonical mnemonics for registers. The register names `$pc` and `$sp` are used for the program counter register and the stack pointer. `$fp` is used for a register that contains a pointer to the current stack frame, and `$ps` is used for a register that contains the processor status. For example, you could print the program counter in hex with

```
p/x $pc
```

or print the instruction to be executed next with

```
x/i $pc
```

or add four to the stack pointer[1] with

```
set $sp += 4
```

Whenever possible, these four standard register names are available on your machine even though the machine has different canonical mnemonics, so long as there is no conflict. The `info registers` command shows the canonical names. For example, on the SPARC, `info registers` displays the processor status register as `$psr` but you can also refer to it as `$ps`.

GDB always considers the contents of an ordinary register as an integer when the register is examined in this way. Some machines have special registers which can hold nothing but floating point; these registers are considered to have floating point values. There is no way to refer to the contents of an ordinary register as floating point value (although you can *print* it as a floating point value with '`print/f $regname`').

Some registers have distinct "raw" and "virtual" data formats. This

---

[1] This is a way of removing one word from the stack, on machines where stacks grow downward in memory (most machines, nowadays). This assumes that the innermost stack frame is selected; setting `$sp` is not allowed when other stack frames are selected. To pop entire frames off the stack, regardless of machine architecture, use `return`; see Section 11.4 [Returning from a Function], page 95.

means that the data format in which the register contents are saved by the operating system is not the same one that your program normally sees. For example, the registers of the 68881 floating point coprocessor are always saved in "extended" (raw) format, but all C programs expect to work with "double" (virtual) format. In such cases, GDB normally works with the virtual format only (the format that makes sense for your program), but the `info registers` command prints the data in both formats.

Normally, register values are relative to the selected stack frame (see Section 6.3 [Selecting a Frame], page 47). This means that you get the value that the register would contain if all stack frames farther in were exited and their saved registers restored. In order to see the true contents of hardware registers, you must select the innermost frame (with 'frame 0').

However, GDB must deduce where registers are saved, from the machine code generated by your compiler. If some registers are not saved, or if GDB is unable to locate the saved registers, the selected stack frame will make no difference.

## 8.11  Floating Point Hardware

Depending on the host machine architecture, GDB may be able to give you more information about the status of the floating point hardware.

`info float`

> If available, provides hardware-dependent information about the floating point unit. The exact contents and layout vary depending on the floating point chip.

# 9  Using GDB with Different Languages

Although programming languages generally have common aspects, they are rarely expressed in the same manner. For instance, in ANSI C, dereferencing a pointer p is accomplished by *p, but in Modula-2, it is accomplished by p^. Values can also be represented (and displayed) differently. Hex numbers in C are written like '0x1ae', while in Modula-2 they appear as '1AEH'.

Language-specific information is built into GDB for some languages, allowing you to express operations like the above in your program's native language, and allowing GDB to output values in a manner consistent with the syntax of your program's native language. The language you use to build expressions, called the *working language*, can be selected manually, or GDB can set it automatically.

## 9.1  Switching Between Source Languages

There are two ways to control the working language—either have GDB set it automatically, or select it manually yourself. You can use the set language command for either purpose. On startup, GDB defaults to setting the language automatically.

### 9.1.1  Setting the Working Language

If you allow GDB to set the language automatically, expressions will be interpreted the same way in your debugging session and your program.

If you wish, you may set the language manually. To do this, issue the command 'set language *lang*', where *lang* is the name of a language: c or modula-2. For a list of the supported languages, type 'set language'.

Setting the language manually prevents GDB from updating the working language automatically. This can lead to confusion if you try to debug a program when the working language is not the same as the source language, when an expression is acceptable to both languages—but means different things. For instance, if the current source file were written in C, and GDB was parsing Modula-2, a command such as:

```
print a = b + c
```

might not have the effect you intended. In C, this means to add b and c and place the result in a. The result printed would be the value of a. In Modula-2, this means to compare a to the result of b+c, yielding a BOOLEAN value.

## 9.1.2  Having GDB Infer the Source Language

To have GDB set the working language automatically, use 'set language local' or 'set language auto'. GDB then infers the language that a program was written in by looking at the name of its source files, and examining their extensions:

'*.mod'        Modula-2 source file

'*.c'

'*.cc'          C or C++ source file.

This information is recorded for each function or procedure in a source file. When your program stops in a frame (usually by encountering a breakpoint), GDB sets the working language to the language recorded for the function in that frame. If the language for a frame is unknown (that is, if the function or block corresponding to the frame was defined in a source file that does not have a recognized extension), the current working language is not changed, and GDB issues a warning.

This may not seem necessary for most programs, which are written entirely in one source language. However, program modules and libraries written in one source language can be used by a main program written in a different source language. Using 'set language auto' in this case frees you from having to set the working language manually.

## 9.2  Displaying the Language

The following commands will help you find out which language is the working language, and also what language source files were written in.

show language

> Display the current working language. This is the language you can use with commands such as print to build and compute expressions that may involve variables in your program.

info frame

> Among the other information listed here (see Section 6.4 [Information about a Frame], page 48) is the source language for this frame. This is the language that will become the working language if you ever use an identifier that is in this frame.

info source

> Among the other information listed here (see Chapter 10 [Examining the Symbol Table], page 89) is the source language of this source file.

## 9.3  Type and Range Checking

> *Warning:* In this release, the GDB commands for type and range checking are included, but they do not yet have any effect. This section documents the intended facilities.

Some languages are designed to guard you against making seemingly common errors through a series of compile- and run-time checks. These include checking the type of arguments to functions and operators, and making sure mathematical overflows are caught at run time. Checks such as these help to ensure a program's correctness once it has been compiled by eliminating type mismatches, and providing active checks for range errors when your program is running.

GDB can check for conditions like the above if you wish. Although GDB will not check the statements in your program, it can check expressions entered directly into GDB for evaluation via the `print` command, for example. As with the working language, GDB can also decide whether or not to check automatically based on your program's source language. See Section 9.4 [Supported Languages], page 77, for the default settings of supported languages.

### 9.3.1  An Overview of Type Checking

Some languages, such as Modula-2, are strongly typed, meaning that the arguments to operators and functions have to be of the correct type, otherwise an error occurs. These checks prevent type mismatch errors from ever causing any run-time problems. For example,

   1 + 2 $\Rightarrow$ 3

but

   $\boxed{\text{error}}$  1 + 2.3

The second example fails because the `CARDINAL` 1 is not type-compatible with the `REAL` 2.3.

For expressions you use in GDB commands, you can tell the GDB type checker to skip checking; to treat any mismatches as errors and abandon the expression; or only issue warnings when type mismatches occur, but evaluate the expression anyway. When you choose the last of these, GDB evaluates expressions like the second example above, but also issues a warning.

Even though you may turn type checking off, other type-based reasons may prevent GDB from evaluating an expression. For instance, GDB does not know how to add an `int` and a `struct foo`. These particular type errors have nothing to do with the language in use, and usually arise from expressions, such as the one described above, which make little sense to evaluate anyway.

Each language defines to what degree it is strict about type. For instance, both Modula-2 and C require the arguments to arithmetical operators to be numbers. In C, enumerated types and pointers can be represented as numbers, so that they are valid arguments to mathematical operators. See Section 9.4 [Supported Languages], page 77, for further details on specific languages.

GDB provides some additional commands for controlling the type checker:

`set check type auto`

> Set type checking on or off based on the current working language. See Section 9.4 [Supported Languages], page 77, for the default settings for each language.

`set check type on`
`set check type off`

> Set type checking on or off, overriding the default setting for the current working language. Issue a warning if the setting does not match the language's default. If any type mismatches occur in evaluating an expression while typechecking is on, GDB prints a message and aborts evaluation of the expression.

`set check type warn`

> Cause the type checker to issue warnings, but to always attempt to evaluate the expression. Evaluating the expression may still be impossible for other reasons. For example, GDB cannot add numbers and structures.

`show type`  Show the current setting of the type checker, and whether or not GDB is setting it automatically.

## 9.3.2 An Overview of Range Checking

In some languages (such as Modula-2), it is an error to exceed the bounds of a type; this is enforced with run-time checks. Such range checking is meant to ensure program correctness by making sure computations do not overflow, or indices on an array element access do not exceed the bounds of the array.

For expressions you use in GDB commands, you can tell GDB to operate in one of three ways on range errors: ignore them, always treat them as errors and abandon the expression, or issue warnings when a range error occurs but evaluate the expression anyway.

A range error can result from numerical overflow, from exceeding an array index bound, or when you type a constant that is not a member of any type. Some languages, however, do not treat overflows as an error. In many implementations of C, mathematical overflow causes the result to "wrap around" to lower values—for example, if $m$ is the largest integer value, and $s$ is the smallest, then

$$m + 1 \Rightarrow s$$

This, too, is specific to individual languages, and in some cases specific to individual compilers or machines. See Section 9.4 [Supported Languages], page 77, for further details on specific languages.

GDB provides some additional commands for controlling the range checker:

**set check range auto**

> Set range checking on or off based on the current working language. See Section 9.4 [Supported Languages], page 77, for the default settings for each language.

**set check range on**
**set check range off**

> Set range checking on or off, overriding the default setting for the current working language. A warning is issued if the setting does not match the language's default. If a range error occurs, then a message is printed and evaluation of the expression is aborted.

**set check range warn**

> Output messages when the GDB range checker detects a range error, but attempt to evaluate the expression anyway. Evaluating the expression may still be impossible for other reasons, such as accessing memory that the process does not own (a typical example from many UNIX systems).

**show range**

> Show the current setting of the range checker, and whether or not it is being set automatically by GDB.

## 9.4 Supported Languages

GDB 4 supports C, C++, and Modula-2. The syntax for C and C++ is so closely related that GDB does not distinguish the two. Some GDB features may be used in expressions regardless of the language you use: the GDB

@ and :: operators, and the '{type}addr' construct (see Section 8.1 [Expressions], page 57) can be used with the constructs of any of the supported languages.

The following sections detail to what degree each of these source languages is supported by GDB. These sections are not meant to be language tutorials or references, but serve only as a reference guide to what the GDB expression parser will accept, and what input and output formats should look like for different languages. There are many good books written on each of these languages; please look to these for a language reference or tutorial.

## 9.4.1  C and C++

Since C and C++ are so closely related, GDB does not distinguish between them when interpreting the expressions recognized in GDB commands.

The C++ debugging facilities are jointly implemented by the GNU C++ compiler and GDB. Therefore, to debug your C++ code effectively, you must compile your C++ programs with the GNU C++ compiler, g++.

### 9.4.1.1  C and C++ Operators

Operators must be defined on values of specific types. For instance, + is defined on numbers, but not on structures. Operators are often defined on groups of types. For the purposes of C and C++, the following definitions hold:

- *Integral types* include int with any of its storage-class specifiers, char, and enums.
- *Floating-point types* include float and double.
- *Pointer types* include all types defined as (*type* *).
- *Scalar types* include all of the above.

The following operators are supported. They are listed here in order of increasing precedence:

,            The comma or sequencing operator. Expressions in a comma-separated list are evaluated from left to right, with the result of the entire expression being the last expression evaluated.

=            Assignment. The value of an assignment expression is the value assigned. Defined on scalar types.

*op=*         Used in an expression of the form *a op= b*, and translated to *a = a op b*. *op=* and = have the same precedence. *op* is any one of the operators |, ^, &, <<, >>, +, -, *, /, %.

?:         The ternary operator. *a ? b : c* can be thought of as: if *a* then *b* else *c*. *a* should be of an integral type.

||         Logical OR. Defined on integral types.

&&         Logical AND. Defined on integral types.

|         Bitwise OR. Defined on integral types.

^         Bitwise exclusive-OR. Defined on integral types.

&         Bitwise AND. Defined on integral types.

==, !=         Equality and inequality. Defined on scalar types. The value of these expressions is 0 for false and non-zero for true.

<, >, <=, >=

        Less than, greater than, less than or equal, greater than or equal. Defined on scalar types. The value of these expressions is 0 for false and non-zero for true.

<<, >>         left shift, and right shift. Defined on integral types.

@         The GDB "artificial array" operator (see Section 8.1 [Expressions], page 57).

+, -         Addition and subtraction. Defined on integral types, floating-point types and pointer types.

*, /, %         Multiplication, division, and modulus. Multiplication and division are defined on integral and floating-point types. Modulus is defined on integral types.

++, --         Increment and decrement. When appearing before a variable, the operation is performed before the variable is used in an expression; when appearing after it, the variable's value is used before the operation takes place.

*         Pointer dereferencing. Defined on pointer types. Same precedence as ++.

&         Address operator. Defined on variables. Same precedence as ++.

-         Negative. Defined on integral and floating-point types. Same precedence as ++.

!         Logical negation. Defined on integral types. Same precedence as ++.

~         Bitwise complement operator. Defined on integral types. Same precedence as ++.

| | |
|---|---|
| ., -> | Structure member, and pointer-to-structure member. For convenience, GDB regards the two as equivalent, choosing whether to dereference a pointer based on the stored type information. Defined on **structs** and **unions**. |
| [] | Array indexing. a[*i*] is defined as *(a+*i*). Same precedence as ->. |
| () | Function parameter list. Same precedence as ->. |
| :: | C++ scope resolution operator. Defined on **struct**, **union**, and **class** types. |
| :: | Doubled colons also stand for the GDB scope operator (see Section 8.1 [Expressions], page 57). Same precedence as ::, above. |

## 9.4.1.2 C and C++ Constants

GDB allows you to express the constants of C and C++ in the following ways:

- Integer constants are a sequence of digits. Octal constants are specified by a leading '0' (ie. zero), and hexadecimal constants by a leading '0x' or '0X'. Constants may also end with a letter 'l', specifying that the constant should be treated as a **long** value.

- Floating point constants are a sequence of digits, followed by a decimal point, followed by a sequence of digits, and optionally followed by an exponent. An exponent is of the form: 'e[[+]|-]*nnn*', where *nnn* is another sequence of digits. The '+' is optional for positive exponents.

- Enumerated constants consist of enumerated identifiers, or their integral equivalents.

- Character constants are a single character surrounded by single quotes ('), or a number—the ordinal value of the corresponding character (usually its ASCII value). Within quotes, the single character may be represented by a letter or by *escape sequences*, which are of the form '\\*nnn*', where *nnn* is the octal representation of the character's ordinal value; or of the form '\\*x*', where '*x*' is a predefined special character—for example, '\n' for newline.

- String constants are a sequence of character constants surrounded by double quotes (").

- Pointer constants are an integral value.

## 9.4.1.3 C++ Expressions

GDB's expression handling has the following extensions to interpret a significant subset of C++ expressions:

1. Member function calls are allowed; you can use expressions like
   ```
   count = aml->GetOriginal(x, y)
   ```

2. While a member function is active (in the selected stack frame), your expressions have the same namespace available as the member function; that is, GDB allows implicit references to the class instance pointer `this` following the same rules as C++.

3. You can call overloaded functions; GDB will resolve the function call to the right definition, with one restriction—you must use arguments of the type required by the function that you want to call. GDB will not perform conversions requiring constructors or user-defined type operators.

4. GDB understands variables declared as C++ references; you can use them in expressions just as you do in C++ source—they are automatically dereferenced.

   In the parameter list shown when GDB displays a frame, the values of reference variables are not displayed (unlike other variables); this avoids clutter, since references are often used for large structures. The *address* of a reference variable is always shown, unless you have specified 'set print address off'.

5. GDB supports the C++ name resolution operator ::—your expressions can use it just as expressions in your program do. Since one scope may be defined in another, you can use :: repeatedly if necessary, for example in an expression like '*scope1* :: *scope2* :: *name*'. GDB also allows resolving name scope by reference to source files, in both C and C++ debugging (see Section 8.2 [Program Variables], page 58).

## 9.4.1.4  C and C++ Defaults

If you allow GDB to set type and range checking automatically, they both default to **off** whenever the working language changes to C/C++. This happens regardless of whether you, or GDB, selected the working language.

If you allow GDB to set the language automatically, it sets the working language to C/C++ on entering code compiled from a source file whose name ends with '.c' or '.cc'. See Section 9.1.2 [Having GDB infer the source language], page 74, for further details.

## 9.4.1.5  C and C++ Type and Range Checks

By default, when GDB parses C or C++ expressions, type checking is not used. However, if you turn type checking on, GDB will consider two variables type equivalent if:

- The two variables are structured and have the same structure, union, or enumerated tag.

- The two variables have the same type name, or types that have been declared equivalent through **typedef**.

Range checking, if turned on, is done on mathematical operations. Array indices are not checked, since they are often used to index a pointer that is not itself an array.

## 9.4.1.6  GDB and C

The **set print union** and **show print union** commands apply to the union type. When set to 'on', any union that is inside a **struct** or **class** will also be printed. Otherwise, it will appear as '{...}'.

The **@** operator aids in the debugging of dynamic arrays, formed with pointers and a memory allocation function. See Section 8.1 [Expressions], page 57.

## 9.4.1.7  GDB Commands for C++

Some GDB commands are particularly useful with C++, and some are designed specifically for use with C++. Here is a summary:

breakpoint menus

> When you want a breakpoint in a function whose name is overloaded, GDB's breakpoint menus help you specify which function definition you want. See Section 5.1.8 [Breakpoint Menus], page 39.

rbreak *regex*

> Setting breakpoints using regular expressions is helpful for setting breakpoints on overloaded functions that are not members of any special classes. See Section 5.1.1 [Setting Breakpoints], page 30.

catch *exceptions*
info catch

> Debug C++ exception handling using these commands. See Section 5.1.3 [Breakpoints and Exceptions], page 32.

`ptype` *typename*

> Print inheritance relationships as well as other information for type *typename*. See Chapter 10 [Examining the Symbol Table], page 89.

`set print demangle`
`show print demangle`
`set print asm-demangle`
`show print asm-demangle`

> Control whether C++ symbols display in their source form, both when displaying code as C++ source and when displaying disassemblies. See Section 8.7 [Print Settings], page 64.

`set print object`
`show print object`

> Choose whether to print derived (actual) or declared types of objects. See Section 8.7 [Print Settings], page 64.

`set print vtbl`
`show print vtbl`

> Control the format for printing virtual function tables. See Section 8.7 [Print Settings], page 64.

## 9.4.2 Modula-2

The extensions made to GDB to support Modula-2 only support output from the GNU Modula-2 compiler (which is currently being developed). Other Modula-2 compilers are not currently supported, and attempting to debug executables produced by them will most likely result in an error as GDB reads in the executable's symbol table.

## 9.4.2.1 Operators

Operators must be defined on values of specific types. For instance, `+` is defined on numbers, but not on structures. Operators are often defined on groups of types. For the purposes of Modula-2, the following definitions hold:

- *Integral types* consist of `INTEGER`, `CARDINAL`, and their subranges.
- *Character types* consist of `CHAR` and its subranges.
- *Floating-point types* consist of `REAL`.
- *Pointer types* consist of anything declared as `POINTER TO` *type*.

- *Scalar types* consist of all of the above.
- *Set types* consist of SETs and BITSETs.
- *Boolean types* consist of BOOLEAN.

The following operators are supported, and appear in order of increasing precedence:

| | |
|---|---|
| , | Function argument or array index separator. |
| := | Assignment. The value of *var* := *value* is *value*. |
| <, > | Less than, greater than on integral, floating-point, or enumerated types. |
| <=, >= | Less than, greater than, less than or equal to, greater than or equal to on integral, floating-point and enumerated types, or set inclusion on set types. Same precedence as <. |
| =, <>, # | Equality and two ways of expressing inequality, valid on scalar types. Same precedence as <. In GDB scripts, only <> is available for inequality, since # conflicts with the script comment character. |
| IN | Set membership. Defined on set types and the types of their members. Same precedence as <. |
| OR | Boolean disjunction. Defined on boolean types. |
| AND, & | Boolean conjunction. Defined on boolean types. |
| @ | The GDB "artificial array" operator (see Section 8.1 [Expressions], page 57). |
| +, - | Addition and subtraction on integral and floating-point types, or union and difference on set types. |
| * | Multiplication on integral and floating-point types, or set intersection on set types. |
| / | Division on floating-point types, or symmetric set difference on set types. Same precedence as *. |
| DIV, MOD | Integer division and remainder. Defined on integral types. Same precedence as *. |
| - | Negative. Defined on INTEGERs and REALs. |
| ^ | Pointer dereferencing. Defined on pointer types. |
| NOT | Boolean negation. Defined on boolean types. Same precedence as ^. |
| . | RECORD field selector. Defined on RECORDs. Same precedence as ^. |
| [] | Array indexing. Defined on ARRAYs. Same precedence as ^. |

()          Procedure argument list. Defined on PROCEDUREs. Same precedence as ^.

::, .       GDB and Modula-2 scope operators.

*Warning:* Sets and their operations are not yet supported, so GDB will treat the use of the operator IN, or the use of operators +, -, *, /, =, <>, #, <=, and >= on sets as an error.

## 9.4.2.2 Built-in Functions and Procedures

Modula-2 also makes available several built-in procedures and functions. In describing these, the following metavariables are used:

a        represents an ARRAY variable.

c        represents a CHAR constant or variable.

i        represents a variable or constant of integral type.

m       represents an identifier that belongs to a set. Generally used in the same function with the metavariable $s$. The type of $s$ should be SET OF mtype (where mtype is the type of $m$.

n        represents a variable or constant of integral or floating-point type.

r        represents a variable or constant of floating-point type.

t        represents a type.

v        represents a variable.

x        represents a variable or constant of one of many types. See the explanation of the function for details.

All Modula-2 built-in procedures also return a result, described below.

ABS($n$)     Returns the absolute value of $n$.

CAP($c$)     If $c$ is a lower case letter, it returns its upper case equivalent, otherwise it returns its argument

CHR($i$)     Returns the character whose ordinal value is $i$.

DEC($v$)     Decrements the value in the variable $v$. Returns the new value.

DEC($v,i$)    Decrements the value in the variable $v$ by $i$. Returns the new value.

EXCL($m,s$)

           Removes the element $m$ from the set $s$. Returns the new set.

FLOAT($i$)   Returns the floating point equivalent of the integer $i$.

HIGH($a$)    Returns the index of the last member of $a$.

INC($v$)     Increments the value in the variable $v$. Returns the new value.

INC(*v*,*i*)     Increments the value in the variable *v* by *i*. Returns the new value.

INCL(*m*,*s*)

     Adds the element *m* to the set *s* if it is not already there. Returns the new set.

MAX(*t*)     Returns the maximum value of the type *t*.

MIN(*t*)     Returns the minimum value of the type *t*.

ODD(*i*)     Returns boolean TRUE if *i* is an odd number.

ORD(*x*)     Returns the ordinal value of its argument. For example, the ordinal value of a character is its ASCII value (on machines supporting the ASCII character set). *x* must be of an ordered type, which include integral, character and enumerated types.

SIZE(*x*)     Returns the size of its argument. *x* can be a variable or a type.

TRUNC(*r*)     Returns the integral part of *r*.

VAL(*t*,*i*)     Returns the member of the type *t* whose ordinal value is *i*.

    *Warning:* Sets and their operations are not yet supported, so GDB will treat the use of procedures INCL and EXCL as an error.

## 9.4.2.3 Constants

GDB allows you to express the constants of Modula-2 in the following ways:

- Integer constants are simply a sequence of digits. When used in an expression, a constant is interpreted to be type-compatible with the rest of the expression. Hexadecimal integers are specified by a trailing 'H', and octal integers by a trailing 'B'.

- Floating point constants appear as a sequence of digits, followed by a decimal point and another sequence of digits. An optional exponent can then be specified, in the form 'E[+|-]*nnn*', where '[+|-]*nnn*' is the desired exponent. All of the digits of the floating point constant must be valid decimal (base 10) digits.

- Character constants consist of a single character enclosed by a pair of like quotes, either single (') or double ("). They may also be expressed by their ordinal value (their ASCII value, usually) followed by a 'C'.

- String constants consist of a sequence of characters enclosed by a pair of like quotes, either single (') or double ("). Escape sequences in the style of C are also allowed. See Section 9.4.1.2 [C and C++ Constants], page 80, for a brief explanation of escape sequences.

- Enumerated constants consist of an enumerated identifier.
- Boolean constants consist of the identifiers TRUE and FALSE.
- Pointer constants consist of integral values only.
- Set constants are not yet supported.

### 9.4.2.4 Modula-2 Defaults

If type and range checking are set automatically by GDB, they both default to on whenever the working language changes to Modula-2. This happens regardless of whether you, or GDB, selected the working language.

If you allow GDB to set the language automatically, then entering code compiled from a file whose name ends with '.mod' will set the working language to Modula-2. See Section 9.1.2 [Having GDB set the language automatically], page 74, for further details.

### 9.4.2.5 Deviations from Standard Modula-2

A few changes have been made to make Modula-2 programs easier to debug. This is done primarily via loosening its type strictness:

- Unlike in standard Modula-2, pointer constants can be formed by integers. This allows you to modify pointer variables during debugging. (In standard Modula-2, the actual address contained in a pointer variable is hidden from you; it can only be modified through direct assignment to another pointer variable or expression that returned a pointer.)
- C escape sequences can be used in strings and characters to represent non-printable characters. GDB will print out strings with these escape sequences embedded. Single non-printable characters are printed using the 'CHR(nnn)' format.
- The assignment operator (:=) returns the value of its right-hand argument.
- All built-in procedures both modify *and* return their argument.

### 9.4.2.6 Modula-2 Type and Range Checks

*Warning:* in this release, GDB does not yet perform type or range checking.

GDB considers two Modula-2 variables type equivalent if:

- They are of types that have been declared equivalent via a TYPE *t1* = *t2* statement

- They have been declared on the same line. (Note: This is true of the GNU Modula-2 compiler, but it may not be true of other compilers.)

As long as type checking is enabled, any attempt to combine variables whose types are not equivalent is an error.

Range checking is done on all mathematical operations, assignment, array index bounds, and all built-in functions and procedures.

### 9.4.2.7  Scope Operators :: (colon-colon) and . (dot)

There are a few subtle differences between the Modula-2 scope operator (.) and the GDB scope operator (::). The two have similar syntax:

> *module* . *id*
> *scope* :: *id*

where *scope* is the name of a module or a procedure, *module* the name of a module, and *id* is any declared identifier within your program, except another module.

Using the :: operator makes GDB search the scope specified by *scope* for the identifier *id*. If it is not found in the specified scope, then GDB will search all scopes enclosing the one specified by *scope*.

Using the . operator makes GDB search the current scope for the identifier specified by *id* that was imported from the definition module specified by *module*. With this operator, it is an error if the identifier *id* was not imported from definition module *module*, or if *id* is not an identifier in *module*.

### 9.4.2.8  GDB and Modula-2

Some GDB commands have little use when debugging Modula-2 programs. Five subcommands of **set print** and **show print** apply specifically to C and C++: 'vtbl', 'demangle', 'asm-demangle', 'object', and 'union'. The first four apply to C++, and the last to C's union type, which has no direct analogue in Modula-2.

The @ operator (see Section 8.1 [Expressions], page 57), while available while using any language, is not useful with Modula-2. Its intent is to aid the debugging of *dynamic* arrays, which cannot be created in Modula-2 as they can in C or C++. However, because an address can be specified by an integral constant, the construct '{*type*}*adrexp*' is still useful. (see Section 8.1 [Expressions], page 57)

In GDB scripts, the Modula-2 inequality operator # is interpreted as the beginning of a comment. Use <> instead.

# 10  Examining the Symbol Table

The commands described in this section allow you to inquire about the symbols (names of variables, functions and types) defined in your program. This information is inherent in the text of your program and does not change as your program executes. GDB finds it in your program's symbol table, in the file indicated when you started GDB (see Section 2.1.1 [Choosing Files], page 13), or by one of the file-management commands (see Section 12.1 [Commands to Specify Files], page 97).

`info address` *symbol*

> Describe where the data for *symbol* is stored. For a register variable, this says which register it is kept in. For a non-register local variable, this prints the stack-frame offset at which the variable is always stored.

> Note the contrast with 'print &*symbol*', which does not work at all for a register variables, and for a stack local variable prints the exact address of the current instantiation of the variable.

`whatis` *exp*

> Print the data type of expression *exp*. *exp* is not actually evaluated, and any side-effecting operations (such as assignments or function calls) inside it do not take place. See Section 8.1 [Expressions], page 57.

`whatis`        Print the data type of $, the last value in the value history.

`ptype` *typename*

> Print a description of data type *typename*. *typename* may be the name of a type, or for C code it may have the form 'struct *struct-tag*', 'union *union-tag*' or 'enum *enum-tag*'.

`ptype` *exp*
`ptype`        Print a description of the type of expression *exp*. `ptype` differs from `whatis` by printing a detailed description, instead of just the name of the type.

> For example, given the following variable declaration:

>     struct complex {double real; double imag;} v;

> compare the output of the two commands:

```
(gdb) whatis v
type = struct complex
(gdb) ptype v
type = struct complex {
    double real;
    double imag;
}
```

As with whatis, using ptype without an argument refers to the type of $, the last value in the value history.

info types *regexp*
info types

> Print a brief description of all types whose name matches *regexp* (or all types in your program, if you supply no argument). Each complete typename is matched as though it were a complete line; thus, 'i type value' gives information on all types in your program whose name includes the string value, but 'i type ^value$' gives information only on types whose complete name is value.
>
> This command differs from ptype in two ways: first, like whatis, it does not print a detailed description; second, it lists all source files where a type is defined.

info source

> Show the name of the current source file—that is, the source file for the function containing the current point of execution—and the language it was written in.

info sources

> Print the names of all source files in your program for which there is debugging information, organized into two lists: files whose symbols have already been read, and files whose symbols will be read when needed.

info functions

> Print the names and data types of all defined functions.

info functions *regexp*

> Print the names and data types of all defined functions whose names contain a match for regular expression *regexp*. Thus, 'info fun step' finds all functions whose names include step; 'info fun ^step' finds those whose names start with step.

info variables

> Print the names and data types of all variables that are declared outside of functions (i.e., excluding local variables).

info variables *regexp*

> Print the names and data types of all variables (except for local

variables) whose names contain a match for regular expression
*regexp*.

**printsyms** *filename*
**printpsyms** *filename*

> Write a dump of debugging symbol data into the file *filename*.
> These commands are used to debug the GDB symbol-reading
> code. Only symbols with debugging data are included. If you
> use **printsyms**, GDB includes all the symbols for which it has al-
> ready collected full details: that is, *filename* reflects symbols for
> only those files whose symbols GDB has read. You can use the
> command **info sources** to find out which files these are. If you
> use **printpsyms**, the dump also shows information about sym-
> bols that GDB only knows partially—that is, symbols defined in
> files that GDB has skimmed, but not yet read completely. The
> description of **symbol-file** describes how GDB reads symbols;
> both commands are described under Section 12.1 [Commands to
> Specify Files], page 97.

# 11  Altering Execution

Once you think you have found an error in your program, you might want to find out for certain whether correcting the apparent error would lead to correct results in the rest of the run. You can find the answer by experiment, using the GDB features for altering execution of the program.

For example, you can store new values into variables or memory locations, give your program a signal, restart it at a different address, or even return prematurely from a function to its caller.

## 11.1  Assignment to Variables

To alter the value of a variable, evaluate an assignment expression. See Section 8.1 [Expressions], page 57. For example,

```
print x=4
```

stores the value 4 into the variable x, and then prints the value of the assignment expression (which is 4). See Chapter 9 [Using GDB with Different Languages], page 73, for more information on operators in supported languages.

If you are not interested in seeing the value of the assignment, use the set command instead of the print command. set is really the same as print except that the expression's value is not printed and is not put in the value history (see Section 8.8 [Value History], page 68). The expression is evaluated only for its effects.

If the beginning of the argument string of the set command appears identical to a set subcommand, use the set variable command instead of just set. This command is identical to set except for its lack of subcommands. For example, if a program has a variable width, you would get an error if you tried to set a new value with set width=13, because GDB already has the command set width.

```
(gdb) whatis width
type = double
(gdb) p width
$4 = 13
(gdb) set width=47
Invalid syntax in expression.
```

The invalid expression, of course, is '=47'. In order to set the program's variable width, use

```
(gdb) set var width=47
```

GDB allows more implicit conversions in assignments than C; you can freely store an integer value into a pointer variable or vice versa, and you can convert any structure to any other structure that is the same length or shorter.

To store values into arbitrary places in memory, use the '{...}' construct to generate a value of specified type at a specified address (see Section 8.1 [Expressions], page 57). For example, {int}0x83040 refers to memory location 0x83040 as an integer (which implies a certain size and representation in memory), and

```
set {int}0x83040 = 4
```

stores the value 4 into that memory location.

## 11.2  Continuing at a Different Address

Ordinarily, when you continue your program, you do so at the place where it stopped, with the continue command. You can instead continue at an address of your own choosing, with the following commands:

jump *linespec*

> Resume execution at line *linespec*. Execution will stop immediately if there is a breakpoint there. See Section 7.1 [Printing Source Lines], page 51, for a description of the different forms of *linespec*.
>
> The jump command does not change the current stack frame, or the stack pointer, or the contents of any memory location or any register other than the program counter. If line *linespec* is in a different function from the one currently executing, the results may be bizarre if the two functions expect different patterns of arguments or of local variables. For this reason, the jump command requests confirmation if the specified line is not in the function currently executing. However, even bizarre results are predictable if you are well acquainted with the machine-language code of your program.

jump *address*

> Resume execution at the instruction at address *address*.

You can get much the same effect as the jump command by storing a new value into the register $pc. The difference is that this does not start your program running; it only changes the address where it *will* run when it is continued. For example,

```
set $pc = 0x485
```

causes the next `continue` command or stepping command to execute at address `0x485`, rather than at the address where your program stopped. See Section 5.2 [Continuing and Stepping], page 40.

The most common occasion to use the `jump` command is to back up, perhaps with more breakpoints set, over a portion of a program that has already executed, in order to examine its execution in more detail.

## 11.3  Giving Your Program a Signal

`signal` *signalnum*

> Resume execution where your program stopped, but give it immediately the signal number *signalnum*.
>
> Alternatively, if *signalnum* is zero, continue execution without giving a signal. This is useful when your program stopped on account of a signal and would ordinary see the signal when resumed with the `continue` command; 'signal 0' causes it to resume without a signal.
>
> `signal` does not repeat when you press RET a second time after executing the command.

## 11.4  Returning from a Function

`return`
`return` *expression*

> You can cancel execution of a function call with the `return` command. If you give an *expression* argument, its value is used as the function's return value.

When you use `return`, GDB discards the selected stack frame (and all frames within it). You can think of this as making the discarded frame return prematurely. If you wish to specify a value to be returned, give that value as the argument to `return`.

This pops the selected stack frame (see Section 6.3 [Selecting a Frame], page 47), and any other frames inside of it, leaving its caller as the innermost remaining frame. That frame becomes selected. The specified value is stored in the registers used for returning values of functions.

The `return` command does not resume execution; it leaves the program stopped in the state that would exist if the function had just returned. In contrast, the `finish` command (see Section 5.2 [Continuing and Stepping], page 40) resumes execution until the selected stack frame returns naturally.

## 11.5  Calling Program Functions

call *expr*   Evaluate the expression *expr* without displaying void returned
              values.

     You can use this variant of the print command if you want to execute
a function from your program, but without cluttering the output with void
returned values. The result is printed and saved in the value history, if it is
not void.

## 11.6  Patching Programs

     By default, GDB opens the file containing your program's executable code
(or the corefile) read-only. This prevents accidental alterations to machine
code; but it also prevents you from intentionally patching your program's
binary.

     If you would like to be able to patch the binary, you can specify that
explicitly with the set write command. For example, you might want to
turn on internal debugging flags, or even to make emergency repairs.

set write on
set write off

              If you specify 'set write on', GDB will open executable and
              core files for both reading and writing; if you specify 'set write
              off' (the default), GDB will open them read-only.

              If you have already loaded a file, you must load it again (us-
              ing the exec-file or core-file command) after changing set
              write, for your new setting to take effect.

show write

              Display whether executable files and core files will be opened for
              writing as well as reading.

# 12  GDB's Files

GDB needs to know the file name of the program to be debugged, both in order to read its symbol table and in order to start your program. To debug a core dump of a previous run, GDB must be told the file name of the core dump.

## 12.1  Commands to Specify Files

The usual way to specify executable and core dump file names is with the command arguments given when you start GDB (see Chapter 2 [Getting In and Out of GDB], page 13).

Occasionally it is necessary to change to a different file during a GDB session. Or you may run GDB and forget to specify the files you want to use. In these situations the GDB commands to specify new files are useful.

`file` *filename*

    Use *filename* as the program to be debugged. It is read for its symbols and for the contents of pure memory. It is also the program executed when you use the `run` command. If you do not specify a directory and the file is not found in GDB's working directory, GDB uses the environment variable `PATH` as a list of directories to search, just as the shell does when looking for a program to run. You can change the value of this variable, for both GDB and your program, using the `path` command.

`file`    `file` with no argument makes GDB discard any information it has on both executable file and the symbol table.

`exec-file` [ *filename* ]

    Specify that the program to be run (but not the symbol table) is found in *filename*. GDB will search the environment variable `PATH` if necessary to locate your program. Omitting *filename* means to discard information on the executable file.

`symbol-file` [ *filename* ]

    Read symbol table information from file *filename*. `PATH` is searched when necessary. Use the `file` command to get both symbol table and program to run from the same file.

    `symbol-file` with no argument clears out GDB's information on your program's symbol table.

    The `symbol-file` command causes GDB to forget the contents of its convenience variables, the value history, and all breakpoints and auto-display expressions. This is because they may contain pointers to the internal data recording symbols and data types, which are part of the old symbol table data being discarded inside GDB.

`symbol-file` will not repeat if you press RET again after executing it once.

On some kinds of object files, the `symbol-file` command does not actually read the symbol table in full right away. Instead, it scans the symbol table quickly to find which source files and which symbols are present. The details are read later, one source file at a time, as they are needed.

The purpose of this two-stage reading strategy is to make GDB start up faster. For the most part, it is invisible except for occasional pauses while the symbol table details for a particular source file are being read. (The `set verbose` command can turn these pauses into messages if desired. See Section 14.6 [Optional Warnings and Messages], page 116.)

When the symbol table is stored in COFF format, `symbol-file` does read the symbol table data in full right away. We have not implemented the two-stage strategy for COFF yet.

When GDB is configured for a particular environment, it will understand debugging information in the standard format generated for that environment; you may use either a GNU compiler, or other compilers that adhere to the local conventions. Best results are usually obtained from GNU compilers; for example, using `gcc` you can generate debugging information for optimized code.

`core-file` [ *filename* ]

Specify the whereabouts of a core dump file to be used as the "contents of memory". Traditionally, core files contain only some parts of the address space of the process that generated them; GDB can access the executable file itself for other parts.

`core-file` with no argument specifies that no core file is to be used.

Note that the core file is ignored when your program is actually running under GDB. So, if you have been running your program and you wish to debug a core file instead, you must kill the subprocess in which the program is running. To do this, use the `kill` command (see Section 4.8 [Killing the Child Process], page 26).

**load** *filename*

> Depending on what remote debugging facilities are configured into GDB, the **load** command may be available. Where it exists, it is meant to make *filename* (an executable) available for debugging on the remote system—by downloading, or dynamic linking, for example. **load** also records *filename*'s symbol table in GDB, like the **add-symbol-file** command.

> If **load** is not available on your GDB, attempting to execute it gets the error message "You can't do that when your target is ..."

> On VxWorks, **load** will dynamically link *filename* on the current target system as well as adding its symbols in GDB.

> With the Nindy interface to an Intel 960 board, **load** will download *filename* to the 960 as well as adding its symbols in GDB.

> **load** will not repeat if you press RET again after using it.

**add-symbol-file** *filename address*

> The **add-symbol-file** command reads additional symbol table information from the file *filename*. You would use this command when *filename* has been dynamically loaded (by some other means) into the program that is running. *address* should be the memory address at which the file has been loaded; GDB cannot figure this out for itself.

> The symbol table of the file *filename* is added to the symbol table originally read with the **symbol-file** command. You can use the **add-symbol-file** command any number of times; the new symbol data thus read keeps adding to the old. To discard all old symbol data instead, use the **symbol-file** command.

> **add-symbol-file** will not repeat if you press RET after using it.

**info files**
**info target**

> **info files** and **info target** are synonymous; both print the current targets (see Chapter 13 [Specifying a Debugging Target], page 103), including the names of the executable and core dump files currently in use by GDB, and the files from which symbols were loaded. The command **help targets** lists all possible targets rather than current ones.

All file-specifying commands allow both absolute and relative file names as arguments. GDB always converts the file name to an absolute path name and remembers it that way.

GDB supports the SunOS shared library format. GDB automatically loads symbol definitions from shared libraries when you use the run command, or when you examine a core file. (Before you issue the run command, GDB will not understand references to a function in a shared library, however—unless you are debugging a core file).

**info share**
**info sharedlibrary**

> Print the names of the shared libraries which are currently loaded.

**sharedlibrary** *regex*
**share** *regex*

> This is an obsolescent command; you can use it to explicitly load shared object library symbols for files matching a UNIX regular expression, but as with files loaded automatically, it will only load shared libraries required by your program for a core file or after typing run. If *regex* is omitted all shared libraries required by your program are loaded.

## 12.2 Errors Reading Symbol Files

While reading a symbol file, GDB will occasionally encounter problems, such as symbol types it does not recognize, or known bugs in compiler output. By default, GDB does not notify you of such problems, since they are relatively common and primarily of interest to people debugging compilers. If you are interested in seeing information about ill-constructed symbol tables, you can either ask GDB to print only one message about each such type of problem, no matter how many times the problem occurs; or you can ask GDB to print more messages, to see how many times the problems occur, with the **set complaints** command (see Section 14.6 [Optional Warnings and Messages], page 116).

The messages currently printed, and their meanings, are:

**inner block not inside outer block in** *symbol*

> The symbol information shows where symbol scopes begin and end (such as at the start of a function or a block of statements). This error indicates that an inner scope block is not fully contained in its outer scope blocks.
>
> GDB circumvents the problem by treating the inner block as if it had the same scope as the outer block. In the error message, *symbol* may be shown as "(don't know)" if the outer block is not a function.

**block at** *address* **out of order**

> The symbol information for symbol scope blocks should occur in order of increasing addresses. This error indicates that it does not do so.
>
> GDB does not circumvent this problem, and will have trouble locating symbols in the source file whose symbol is being read. (You can often determine what source file is affected by specifying **set verbose on**. See Section 14.6 [Optional Warnings and Messages], page 116.)

**bad block start address patched**

> The symbol information for a symbol scope block has a start address smaller than the address of the preceding source line. This is known to occur in the SunOS 4.1.1 (and earlier) C compiler.
>
> GDB circumvents the problem by treating the symbol scope block as starting on the previous source line.

**bad string table offset in symbol** *n*

> Symbol number *n* contains a pointer into the string table which is larger than the size of the string table.
>
> GDB circumvents the problem by considering the symbol to have the name **foo**, which may cause other problems if many symbols end up with this name.

**unknown symbol type 0x**nn

> The symbol information contains new data types that GDB does not yet know how to read. **0x**nn is the symbol type of the misunderstood information, in hexadecimal.
>
> GDB circumvents the error by ignoring this symbol information. This will usually allow your program to be debugged, though certain symbols will not be accessible. If you encounter such a problem and feel like debugging it, you can debug **gdb** with itself, breakpoint on **complain**, then go up to the function **read_dbx_symtab** and examine **\*bufp** to see the symbol.

**stub type has NULL name**

> GDB could not find the full definition for a struct or class.

**const/volatile indicator missing (ok if using g++ v1.x), got...**

> The symbol information for a C++ member function is missing some information that recent versions of the compiler should have output for it.

**info mismatch between compiler and debugger**

> GDB could not parse a type specification output by the compiler.

# 13  Specifying a Debugging Target

A *target* is the execution environment occupied by your program. Often, GDB runs in the same host environment as your program; in that case, the debugging target is specified as a side effect when you use the `file` or `core` commands. When you need more flexibility—for example, running GDB on a physically separate host, or controlling a standalone system over a serial port or a realtime system over a TCP/IP connection—you can use the `target` command to specify one of the target types configured for GDB (see Section 13.2 [Commands for Managing Targets], page 103).

## 13.1  Active Targets

There are three classes of targets: processes, core files, and executable files. GDB can work concurrently on up to three active targets, one in each class. This allows you to (for example) start a process and inspect its activity without abandoning your work on a core file.

For example, if you execute 'gdb a.out', then the executable file a.out is the only active target. If you designate a core file as well—presumably from a prior run that crashed and coredumped—then GDB has two active targets and will use them in tandem, looking first in the corefile target, then in the executable file, to satisfy requests for memory addresses. (Typically, these two classes of target are complementary, since core files contain only a program's read-write memory—variables and so on—plus machine status, while executable files contain only the program text and initialized data.)

When you type `run`, your executable file becomes an active process target as well. When a process target is active, all GDB commands requesting memory addresses refer to that target; addresses in an active core file or executable file target are obscured while the process target is active.

Use the `core-file` and `exec-file` commands to select a new core file or executable target (see Section 12.1 [Commands to Specify Files], page 97). To specify as a target a process that is already running, use the `attach` command (see Section 4.7 [Debugging an Already-Running Process], page 26).

## 13.2  Commands for Managing Targets

Here are commands for managing targets:

`target` *type parameters*

> Connects the GDB host environment to a target machine or process. A target is typically a protocol for talking to debugging

facilities. You use the argument *type* to specify the type or protocol of the target machine.

Further *parameters* are interpreted by the target protocol, but typically include things like device names or host names to connect with, process numbers, and baud rates.

The `target` command will not repeat if you press RET again after executing the command.

`help target`

> Displays the names of all targets available. To display targets currently selected, use either `info target` or `info files` (see Section 12.1 [Commands to Specify Files], page 97).

`help target` *name*

> Describe a particular target, including any parameters necessary to select it.

Here are some common targets (available, or not, depending on the GDB configuration):

`target exec` *prog*

> An executable file. '`target exec` *prog*' is the same as '`exec-file` *prog*'.

`target core` *filename*

> A core dump file. '`target core` *filename*' is the same as '`core-file` *filename*'.

`target remote` *dev*

> Remote serial target in GDB-specific protocol. The argument *dev* specifies what serial device to use for the connection (e.g. '`/dev/ttya`'). See Section 13.3 [Remote Debugging], page 105.

`target amd-eb` *dev speed PROG*

> Remote PC-resident AMD EB29K board, attached over serial lines. *dev* is the serial device, as for `target remote`; *speed* allows you to specify the linespeed; and *PROG* is the name of the program to be debugged, as it appears to DOS on the PC. See Section 13.3.2 [GDB with a Remote EB29K], page 107.

`target nindy` *devicename*

> An Intel 960 board controlled by a Nindy Monitor. *devicename* is the name of the serial device to use for the connection, e.g. '`/dev/ttya`'. See Section 13.3.1 [GDB with a Remote i960 (Nindy)], page 106.

`target vxworks` *machinename*

> A VxWorks system, attached via TCP/IP. The argument *machinename* is the target system's machine name or IP address. See Section 13.3.3 [GDB and VxWorks], page 110.

Different targets are available on different configurations of GDB; your configuration may have more or fewer targets.

## 13.3  Remote Debugging

If you are trying to debug a program running on a machine that cannot run GDB in the usual way, it is often useful to use remote debugging. For example, you might use remote debugging on an operating system kernel, or on a small system which does not have a general purpose operating system powerful enough to run a full-featured debugger.

Some configurations of GDB have special serial or TCP/IP interfaces to make this work with particular debugging targets. In addition, GDB comes with a generic serial protocol (specific to GDB, but not specific to any particular target system) which you can use if you write the remote stubs—the code that will run on the remote system to communicate with GDB.

To use the GDB remote serial protocol, the program to be debugged on the remote machine needs to contain a debugging stub which talks to GDB over the serial line. Several working remote stubs are distributed with GDB; see the 'README' file in the GDB distribution for more information.

For details of this communication protocol, see the comments in the GDB source file 'remote.c'.

To start remote debugging, first run GDB and specify as an executable file the program that is running in the remote machine. This tells GDB how to find your program's symbols and the contents of its pure text. Then establish communication using the `target remote` command with a device name as an argument. For example:

    target remote /dev/ttyb

if the serial line is connected to the device named '/dev/ttyb'. This will stop the remote machine if it is not already stopped.

Now you can use all the usual commands to examine and change data and to step and continue the remote program.

To resume the remote program and stop debugging it, use the `detach` command.

Other remote targets may be available in your configuration of GDB; use help `targets` to list them.

## 13.3.1  GDB with a Remote i960 (Nindy)

*Nindy* is a ROM Monitor program for Intel 960 target systems. When GDB is configured to control a remote Intel 960 using Nindy, you can tell GDB how to connect to the i960 in several ways:

- Through command line options specifying serial port, version of the Nindy protocol, and communications speed;
- By responding to a prompt on startup;
- By using the `target` command at any point during your GDB session. See Section 13.2 [Commands for Managing Targets], page 103.

### 13.3.1.1  Startup with Nindy

If you simply start GDB without using any command-line options, you are prompted for what serial port to use, *before* you reach the ordinary GDB prompt:

```
Attach /dev/ttyNN -- specify NN, or "quit" to quit:
```

Respond to the prompt with whatever suffix (after '`/dev/tty`') identifies the serial port you want to use. You can, if you choose, simply start up with no Nindy connection by responding to the prompt with an empty line. If you do this and later wish to attach to Nindy, use `target` (see Section 13.2 [Commands for Managing Targets], page 103).

### 13.3.1.2  Options for Nindy

These are the startup options for beginning your GDB session with a Nindy-960 board attached:

-r *port*      Specify the serial port name of a serial interface to be used to connect to the target system. This option is only available when GDB is configured for the Intel 960 target architecture. You may specify *port* as any of: a full pathname (e.g. '`-r /dev/ttya`'), a device name in '`/dev`' (e.g. '`-r ttya`'), or simply the unique suffix for a specific `tty` (e.g. '`-r a`').

-O             (An uppercase letter "O", not a zero.) Specify that GDB should use the "old" Nindy monitor protocol to connect to the target system. This option is only available when GDB is configured for the Intel 960 target architecture.

> *Warning:* if you specify '-O', but are actually trying to connect to a target system that expects the newer protocol, the connection will fail, appearing to be a speed mismatch. GDB will repeatedly attempt to re-connect at several different line speeds. You can abort this process with an interrupt.

-brk      Specify that GDB should first send a BREAK signal to the target system, in an attempt to reset it, before connecting to a Nindy target.

> *Warning:* Many target systems do not have the hardware that this requires; it only works with a few boards.

The standard '-b' option controls the line speed used on the serial port.

### 13.3.1.3 Nindy Reset Command

reset     For a Nindy target, this command sends a "break" to the remote target system; this is only useful if the target has been equipped with a circuit to perform a hard reset (or some other interesting action) when a break is detected.

## 13.3.2 GDB with a Remote EB29K

To use GDB from a Unix system to run programs on AMD's EB29K board in a PC, you must first connect a serial cable between the PC and a serial port on the Unix system. In the following, we assume you've hooked the cable between the PC's 'COM1' port and '/dev/ttya' on the Unix system.

### 13.3.2.1 Communications Setup

The next step is to set up the PC's port, by doing something such as the following in DOS on the PC:

```
C:\> MODE com1:9600,n,8,1,none
```

This example—run on an MS DOS 4.0 system—sets the PC port to 9600 bps, no parity, eight data bits, one stop bit, and no "retry" action; you must match the communications parameters when establishing the Unix end of the connection as well.

To give control of the PC to the Unix side of the serial line, type the following at the DOS console:

```
C:\> CTTY com1
```

(Later, if you wish to return control to the DOS console, you can use the command CTTY con—but you must send it over the device that had control, in our example over the 'COM1' serial line).

From the Unix host, use a communications program such as tip or cu to communicate with the PC; for example,

```
cu -s 9600 -l /dev/ttya
```

The cu options shown specify, respectively, the linespeed and the serial port to use. If you use tip instead, your command line may look something like the following:

```
tip -9600 /dev/ttya
```

Your system may define a different name where our example uses '/dev/ttya' as the argument to tip. The communications parameters, including which port to use, are associated with the tip argument in the "remote" descriptions file—normally the system table '/etc/remote'.

Using the tip or cu connection, change the DOS working directory to the directory containing a copy of your 29K program, then start the PC program EBMON (an EB29K control program supplied with your board by AMD). You should see an initial display from EBMON similar to the one that follows, ending with the EBMON prompt '#':

```
C:\> G:

G:\> CD \usr\joe\work29k

G:\USR\JOE\WORK29K> EBMON
Am29000 PC Coprocessor Board Monitor, version 3.0-18
Copyright 1990 Advanced Micro Devices, Inc.
Written by Gibbons and Associates, Inc.

Enter '?' or 'H' for help

PC Coprocessor Type    = EB29K
I/O Base               = 0x208
Memory Base            = 0xd0000

Data Memory Size       = 2048KB
Available I-RAM Range  = 0x8000 to 0x1fffff
Available D-RAM Range  = 0x80002000 to 0x801fffff

PageSize               = 0x400
```

```
Register Stack Size    = 0x800
Memory Stack Size      = 0x1800

CPU PRL                = 0x3
Am29027 Available      = No
Byte Write Available   = Yes

# ~.
```

Then exit the `cu` or `tip` program (done in the example by typing `~.` at the `EBMON` prompt). EBMON will keep running, ready for GDB to take over.

For this example, we've assumed what is probably the most convenient way to make sure the same 29K program is on both the PC and the Unix system: a PC/NFS connection that establishes "drive `G:`" on the PC as a file system on the Unix host. If you do not have PC/NFS or something similar connecting the two systems, you must arrange some other way—perhaps floppy-disk transfer—of getting the 29K program from the Unix system to the PC; GDB will *not* download it over the serial line.

### 13.3.2.2 EB29K Cross-debugging

Finally, `cd` to the directory containing an image of your 29K program on the Unix system, and start GDB—specifying as argument the name of your 29K program:

```
cd /usr/joe/work29k
gdb myfoo
```

Now you can use the `target` command:

```
target amd-eb /dev/ttya 9600 MYFOO
```

In this example, we've assumed your program is in a file called 'myfoo'. Note that the filename given as the last argument to `target amd-eb` should be the name of the program as it appears to DOS. In our example this is simply `MYFOO`, but in general it can include a DOS path, and depending on your transfer mechanism may not resemble the name on the Unix side.

At this point, you can set any breakpoints you wish; when you are ready to see your program run on the 29K board, use the GDB command `run`.

To stop debugging the remote program, use the GDB `detach` command.

To return control of the PC to its console, use `tip` or `cu` once again, after your GDB session has concluded, to attach to `EBMON`. You can then type the command `q` to shut down EBMON, returning control to the DOS command-line interpreter. Type `CTTY con` to return command input to the main DOS console, and type `~.` to leave `tip` or `cu`.

### 13.3.2.3  Remote Log

The `target amd-eb` command creates a file 'eb.log' in the current working directory, to help debug problems with the connection. 'eb.log' records
all the output from EBMON, including echoes of the commands sent to it.
Running 'tail -f' on this file in another window often helps to understand
trouble with EBMON, or unexpected events on the PC side of the connection.

## 13.3.3  GDB and VxWorks

GDB enables developers to spawn and debug tasks running on networked
VxWorks targets from a Unix host. Already-running tasks spawned from the
VxWorks shell can also be debugged. GDB uses code that runs on both the
UNIX host and on the VxWorks target. The program `gdb` is installed and
executed on the UNIX host.

The remote debugging interface (RDB) routines are installed and executed on the VxWorks target. These routines are included in the VxWorks
library 'rdb.a' and are incorporated into the system image when source-level
debugging is enabled in the VxWorks configuration.

If you wish, you can define INCLUDE_RDB in the VxWorks configuration file
'configAll.h' to include the RDB interface routines and spawn the source
debugging task `tRdbTask` when VxWorks is booted. For more information
on configuring and remaking VxWorks, see the manufacturer's manual.

Once you have included the RDB interface in your VxWorks system image
and set your Unix execution search path to find GDB, you are ready to run
GDB. From your UNIX host, type:

    % gdb

GDB will come up showing the prompt:

    (gdb)

### 13.3.3.1  Connecting to VxWorks

The GDB command `target` lets you connect to a VxWorks target on the
network. To connect to a target whose host name is "tt", type:

    (gdb) target vxworks tt

GDB will display a message similar to the following:

    Attaching remote machine across net... Success!

GDB will then attempt to read the symbol tables of any object modules
loaded into the VxWorks target since it was last booted. GDB locates these

files by searching the directories listed in the command search path (see Section 4.4 [Your Program's Environment], page 23); if it fails to find an object file, it will display a message such as:

    prog.o: No such file or directory.

This will cause the `target` command to abort. When this happens, you should add the appropriate directory to the search path, with the GDB command `path`, and execute the `target` command again.

### 13.3.3.2 VxWorks Download

If you have connected to the VxWorks target and you want to debug an object that has not yet been loaded, you can use the GDB `load` command to download a file from UNIX to VxWorks incrementally. The object file given as an argument to the `load` command is actually opened twice: first by the VxWorks target in order to download the code, then by GDB in order to read the symbol table. This can lead to problems if the current working directories on the two systems differ. It is simplest to set the working directory on both systems to the directory in which the object file resides, and then to reference the file by its name, without any path. Thus, to load a program 'prog.o', residing in 'wherever/vw/demo/rdb', on VxWorks type:

    -> cd "wherever/vw/demo/rdb"

On GDB type:

    (gdb) cd wherever/vw/demo/rdb
    (gdb) load prog.o

GDB will display a response similar to the following:

    Reading symbol data from wherever/vw/demo/rdb/prog.o... done.

You can also use the `load` command to reload an object module after editing and recompiling the corresponding source file. Note that this will cause GDB to delete all currently-defined breakpoints, auto-displays, and convenience variables, and to clear the value history. (This is necessary in order to preserve the integrity of debugger data structures that reference the target system's symbol table.)

### 13.3.3.3 Running Tasks

You can also attach to an existing task using the `attach` command as follows:

    (gdb) attach task

where *task* is the VxWorks hexadecimal task ID. The task can be running or suspended when you attach to it. If running, it will be suspended at the time of attachment.

# 14  Controlling GDB

You can alter many aspects of GDB's interaction with you by using the `set` command. For commands controlling how GDB displays data, see Section 8.7 [Print Settings], page 64; other settings are described here.

## 14.1  Prompt

GDB indicates its readiness to read a command by printing a string called the *prompt*. This string is normally '(gdb)'. You can change the prompt string with the `set prompt` command. For instance, when debugging GDB with GDB, it is useful to change the prompt in one of the GDBs so that you can always tell which one you are talking to.

`set prompt` *newprompt*

> Directs GDB to use *newprompt* as its prompt string henceforth.

`show prompt`

> Prints a line of the form: 'GDB's prompt is: *your-prompt*'

## 14.2  Command Editing

GDB reads its input commands via the *readline* interface. This GNU library provides consistent behavior for programs which provide a command line interface to the user. Advantages are `emacs`-style or `vi`-style inline editing of commands, `csh`-like history substitution, and a storage and recall of command history across debugging sessions.

You may control the behavior of command line editing in GDB with the command `set`.

`set editing`
`set editing on`

> Enable command line editing (enabled by default).

`set editing off`

> Disable command line editing.

`show editing`

> Show whether command line editing is enabled.

## 14.3  Command History

Here are commands for handling the command history:

`set history filename` *fname*

Set the name of the GDB command history file to *fname*. This
is the file from which GDB will read an initial command history list or to which it will write this list when it exits. This
list is accessed through history expansion or through the history command editing characters listed below. This file defaults
to the value of the environment variable GDBHISTFILE, or to
'`./.gdb_history`' if this variable is not set.

`set history save`
`set history save on`

Record command history in a file, whose name may be specified
with the `set history filename` command. By default, this option is disabled.

`set history save off`

Stop recording command history in a file.

`set history size` *size*

Set the number of commands which GDB will keep in its history list. This defaults to the value of the environment variable
HISTSIZE, or to 256 if this variable is not set.

History expansion assigns special meaning to the character !.

See Section B.2.1 [Event Designators], page 142.

Since ! is also the logical not operator in C, history expansion is off by
default. If you decide to enable history expansion with the `set history`
`expansion on` command, you may sometimes need to follow ! (when it is
used as logical not, in an expression) with a space or a tab to prevent it from
being expanded. The readline history facilities will not attempt substitution
on the strings != and !(, even when history expansion is enabled.

The commands to control history expansion are:

`set history expansion on`
`set history expansion`

Enable history expansion. History expansion is off by default.

`set history expansion off`

Disable history expansion.

The readline code comes with more complete documentation of
editing and history expansion features. Users unfamiliar with

emacs or vi may wish to read it. See Appendix A [Command
Line Editing], page 131.

`show history`
`show history filename`
`show history save`
`show history size`
`show history expansion`

These commands display the state of the GDB history parameters. show history by itself displays all four states.

`show commands`

Display the last ten commands in the command history.

`show commands n`

Print ten commands centered on command number n.

`show commands +`

Print ten commands just after the commands last printed.

## 14.4 Screen Size

Certain commands to GDB may produce large amounts of information
output to the screen. To help you read all of it, GDB pauses and asks you
for input at the end of each page of output. Type RET when you want to
continue the output. GDB also uses the screen width setting to determine
when to wrap lines of output. Depending on what is being printed, it tries
to break the line at a readable place, rather than simply letting it overflow
onto the following line.

Normally GDB knows the size of the screen from the termcap data base
together with the value of the TERM environment variable and the stty rows
and stty cols settings. If this is not correct, you can override it with the
set height and set width commands:

`set height lpp`
`show height`
`set width cpl`
`show width`

These set commands specify a screen height of lpp lines and a
screen width of cpl characters. The associated show commands
display the current settings.

If you specify a height of zero lines, GDB will not pause during
output no matter how long the output is. This is useful if output
is to a file or to an editor buffer.

## 14.5  Numbers

You can always enter numbers in octal, decimal, or hexadecimal in GDB by the usual conventions: octal numbers begin with '0', decimal numbers end with '.', and hexadecimal numbers begin with '0x'. Numbers that begin with none of these are, by default, entered in base 10; likewise, the default display for numbers—when no particular format is specified—is base 10. You can change the default base for both input and output with the `set radix` command.

`set radix` *base*

> Set the default base for numeric input and display. Supported choices for *base* are decimal 2, 8, 10, 16. *base* must itself be specified either unambiguously or using the current default radix; for example, any of
>
> ```
> set radix 1010
> set radix 012
> set radix 10.
> set radix 0xa
> ```
>
> will set the base to decimal. On the other hand, 'set radix 10' will leave the radix unchanged no matter what it was.

`show radix`

> Display the current default base for numeric input and display.

## 14.6  Optional Warnings and Messages

By default, GDB is silent about its inner workings. If you are running on a slow machine, you may want to use the `set verbose` command. It will make GDB tell you when it does a lengthy internal operation, so you will not think it has crashed.

Currently, the messages controlled by `set verbose` are those which announce that the symbol table for a source file is being read (see Section 12.1 [Commands to Specify Files], page 97, in the description of the command `symbol-file`).

`set verbose on`

> Enables GDB's output of certain informational messages.

`set verbose off`

> Disables GDB's output of certain informational messages.

`show verbose`

> Displays whether `set verbose` is on or off.

By default, if GDB encounters bugs in the symbol table of an object file, it is silent; but if you are debugging a compiler, you may find this information useful (see Section 12.2 [Errors Reading Symbol Files], page 100).

`set complaints` *limit*

> Permits GDB to output *limit* complaints about each type of unusual symbols before becoming silent about the problem. Set *limit* to zero to suppress all complaints; set it to a large number to prevent complaints from being suppressed.

`show complaints`

> Displays how many symbol complaints GDB is permitted to produce.

By default, GDB is cautious, and asks what sometimes seem to be a lot of stupid questions to confirm certain commands. For example, if you try to run a program which is already running:

```
(gdb) run
The program being debugged has been started already.
Start it from the beginning? (y or n)
```

If you are willing to unflinchingly face the consequences of your own commands, you can disable this "feature":

`set confirm off`

> Disables confirmation requests.

`set confirm on`

> Enables confirmation requests (the default).

`show confirm`

> Displays state of confirmation requests.

Some systems allow individual object files that make up your program to be replaced without stopping and restarting your program. For example, in VxWorks you can simply recompile a defective object file and keep on running. If you are running on one of these systems, you can allow GDB to reload the symbols for automatically relinked modules:

`set symbol-reloading on`

> Replace symbol definitions for the corresponding source file when an object file with a particular name is seen again.

`set symbol-reloading off`

> Do not replace symbol definitions when re-encountering object

files of the same name.  This is the default state; if you are
not running on a system that permits automatically relinking
modules, you should leave `symbol-reloading` off, since otherwise GDB may discard symbols when linking large programs,
that may contain several modules (from different directories or
libraries) with the same name.

`show symbol-reloading`

Show the current on or off setting.

# 15  Canned Sequences of Commands

Aside from breakpoint commands (see Section 5.1.7 [Breakpoint Command Lists], page 37), GDB provides two ways to store sequences of commands for execution as a unit: user-defined commands and command files.

## 15.1  User-Defined Commands

A *user-defined command* is a sequence of GDB commands to which you assign a new name as a command. This is done with the **define** command.

**define** *commandname*

> Define a command named *commandname*. If there is already a command by that name, you are asked to confirm that you want to redefine it.
>
> The definition of the command is made up of other GDB command lines, which are given following the **define** command. The end of these commands is marked by a line containing **end**.

**document** *commandname*

> Give documentation to the user-defined command *commandname*. The command *commandname* must already be defined. This command reads lines of documentation just as **define** reads the lines of the command definition, ending with **end**. After the **document** command is finished, **help** on command *commandname* will print the documentation you have specified.
>
> You may use the **document** command again to change the documentation of a command. Redefining the command with **define** does not change the documentation.

**help user-defined**

> List all user-defined commands, with the first line of the documentation (if any) for each.

**info user**
**info user** *commandname*

> Display the GDB commands used to define *commandname* (but not its documentation). If no *commandname* is given, display the definitions for all user-defined commands.

User-defined commands do not take arguments. When they are executed, the commands of the definition are not printed. An error in any command stops execution of the user-defined command.

Commands that would ask for confirmation if used interactively proceed without asking when used inside a user-defined command. Many GDB commands that normally print messages to say what they are doing omit the messages when used in a user-defined command.

## 15.2  Command Files

A command file for GDB is a file of lines that are GDB commands. Comments (lines starting with #) may also be included. An empty line in a command file does nothing; it does not mean to repeat the last command, as it would from the terminal.

When you start GDB, it automatically executes commands from its *init files*. These are files named '.gdbinit'. GDB reads the init file (if any) in your home directory and then the init file (if any) in the current working directory. (The init files are not executed if you use the '-nx' option; see Section 2.1.2 [Choosing Modes], page 14.) You can also request the execution of a command file with the source command:

source *filename*

          Execute the command file *filename*.

The lines in a command file are executed sequentially. They are not printed as they are executed. An error in any command terminates execution of the command file.

Commands that would ask for confirmation if used interactively proceed without asking when used in a command file. Many GDB commands that normally print messages to say what they are doing omit the messages when called from command files.

## 15.3  Commands for Controlled Output

During the execution of a command file or a user-defined command, normal GDB output is suppressed; the only output that appears is what is explicitly printed by the commands in the definition. This section describes three commands useful for generating exactly the output you want.

echo *text*   Print *text*. Nonprinting characters can be included in *text* using C escape sequences, such as '\n' to print a newline. **No newline will be printed unless you specify one.** In addition to the standard C escape sequences, a backslash followed by a space stands for a space. This is useful for outputting a string with spaces at the beginning or the end, since leading and trailing spaces are otherwise trimmed from all arguments. Thus, to print ' and foo = ', use the command 'echo \ and foo = \ '.

A backslash at the end of *text* can be used, as in C, to continue the command onto subsequent lines. For example,

```
echo This is some text\n\
which is continued\n\
onto several lines.\n
```

produces the same output as

```
echo This is some text\n
echo which is continued\n
echo onto several lines.\n
```

**output** *expression*

Print the value of *expression* and nothing but that value: no newlines, no '$*nn* = '. The value is not entered in the value history either. See Section 8.1 [Expressions], page 57, for more information on expressions.

**output/***fmt* *expression*

Print the value of *expression* in format *fmt*. You can use the same formats as for `print`. See Section 8.4 [Output Formats], page 60, for more information.

**printf** *string, expressions...*

Print the values of the *expressions* under the control of *string*. The *expressions* are separated by commas and may be either numbers or pointers. Their values are printed as specified by *string*, exactly as if your program were to execute

```
printf (string, expressions...);
```

For example, you can print two values in hex like this:

```
printf "foo, bar-foo = 0x%x, 0x%x\n", foo, bar-
foo
```

The only backslash-escape sequences that you can use in the format string are the simple ones that consist of backslash followed by a letter.

# 16  Using GDB under GNU Emacs

A special interface allows you to use GNU Emacs to view (and edit) the source files for the program you are debugging with GDB.

To use this interface, use the command **M-x gdb** in Emacs. Give the executable file you want to debug as an argument. This command starts GDB as a subprocess of Emacs, with input and output through a newly created Emacs buffer.

Using GDB under Emacs is just like using GDB normally except for two things:

- All "terminal" input and output goes through the Emacs buffer.

This applies both to GDB commands and their output, and to the input and output done by the program you are debugging.

This is useful because it means that you can copy the text of previous commands and input them again; you can even use parts of the output in this way.

All the facilities of Emacs' Shell mode are available for interacting with your program. In particular, you can send signals the usual way—for example, **C-c C-c** for an interrupt, **C-c C-z** for a stop.

- GDB displays source code through Emacs.

Each time GDB displays a stack frame, Emacs automatically finds the source file for that frame and puts an arrow ('=>') at the left margin of the current line. Emacs uses a separate buffer for source display, and splits the window to show both your GDB session and the source.

Explicit GDB **list** or search commands still produce output as usual, but you probably will have no reason to use them.

> *Warning:* If the directory where your program resides is not your current directory, it can be easy to confuse Emacs about the location of the source files, in which case the auxiliary display buffer will not appear to show your source. GDB can find programs by searching your environment's **PATH** variable, so the GDB input and output session will proceed normally; but Emacs does not get enough information back from GDB to locate the source files in this situation. To avoid this problem, either start GDB mode from the directory where your program resides, or specify a full path name when prompted for the **M-x gdb** argument.
>
> A similar confusion can result if you use the GDB **file** command to switch to debugging a program in some other location, from an existing GDB buffer in Emacs.

By default, `M-x gdb` calls the program called 'gdb'. If you need to call GDB by a different name (for example, if you keep several configurations around, with different names) you can set the Emacs variable `gdb-command-name`; for example,

    (setq gdb-command-name "mygdb")

(preceded by `ESC ESC`, or typed in the `*scratch*` buffer, or in your '.emacs' file) will make Emacs call the program named "`mygdb`" instead.

In the GDB I/O buffer, you can use these special Emacs commands in addition to the standard Shell mode commands:

`C-h m`     Describe the features of Emacs' GDB Mode.

`M-s`       Execute to another source line, like the GDB `step` command; also update the display window to show the current file and location.

`M-n`       Execute to next source line in this function, skipping all function calls, like the GDB `next` command. Then update the display window to show the current file and location.

`M-i`       Execute one instruction, like the GDB `stepi` command; update display window accordingly.

`M-x gdb-nexti`

        Execute to next instruction, using the GDB `nexti` command; update display window accordingly.

`C-c C-f`   Execute until exit from the selected stack frame, like the GDB `finish` command.

`M-c`       Continue execution of your program, like the GDB `continue` command.

        *Warning:* In Emacs v19, this command is `C-c C-p`.

`M-u`       Go up the number of frames indicated by the numeric argument (see section "Numeric Arguments" in *The GNU Emacs Manual*), like the GDB `up` command.

        *Warning:* In Emacs v19, this command is `C-c C-u`.

`M-d`       Go down the number of frames indicated by the numeric argument, like the GDB `down` command.

        *Warning:* In Emacs v19, this command is `C-c C-d`.

`C-x &`     Read the number where the cursor is positioned, and insert it at the end of the GDB I/O buffer. For example, if you wish to disassemble code around an address that was displayed earlier, type `disassemble`; then move the cursor to the address display, and pick up the argument for `disassemble` by typing `C-x &`.

You can customize this further on the fly by defining elements of the list `gdb-print-command`; once it is defined, you can format or otherwise process numbers picked up by `C-x &` before they are inserted. A numeric argument to `C-x &` will both indicate that you wish special formatting, and act as an index to pick an element of the list. If the list element is a string, the number to be inserted is formatted using the Emacs function `format`; otherwise the number is passed as an argument to the corresponding list element.

In any source file, the Emacs command `C-x SPC` (`gdb-break`) tells GDB to set a breakpoint on the source line point is on.

If you accidentally delete the source-display buffer, an easy way to get it back is to type the command `f` in the GDB buffer, to request a frame display; when you run under Emacs, this will recreate the source buffer if necessary to show you the context of the current frame.

The source files displayed in Emacs are in ordinary Emacs buffers which are visiting the source files in the usual way. You can edit the files with these buffers if you wish; but keep in mind that GDB communicates with Emacs in terms of line numbers. If you add or delete lines from the text, the line numbers that GDB knows will cease to correspond properly with the code.

# 17  Reporting Bugs in GDB

Your bug reports play an essential role in making GDB reliable.

Reporting a bug may help you by bringing a solution to your problem, or it may not. But in any case the principal function of a bug report is to help the entire community by making the next version of GDB work better. Bug reports are your contribution to the maintenance of GDB.

In order for a bug report to serve its purpose, you must include the information that enables us to fix the bug.

## 17.1  Have You Found a Bug?

If you are not sure whether you have found a bug, here are some guidelines:

- If the debugger gets a fatal signal, for any input whatever, that is a GDB bug. Reliable debuggers never crash.
- If GDB produces an error message for valid input, that is a bug.
- If GDB does not produce an error message for invalid input, that is a bug. However, you should note that your idea of "invalid input" might be our idea of "an extension" or "support for traditional practice".
- If you are an experienced user of debugging tools, your suggestions for improvement of GDB are welcome in any case.

## 17.2  How to Report Bugs

A number of companies and individuals offer support for GNU products. If you obtained GDB from a support organization, we recommend you contact that organization first.

You can find contact information for many support companies and individuals in the file 'etc/SERVICE' in the GNU Emacs distribution.

In any event, we also recommend that you send bug reports for GDB to one of these addresses:

```
bug-gdb@prep.ai.mit.edu
{ucbvax|mit-eddie|uunet}!prep.ai.mit.edu!bug-gdb
```

**Do not send bug reports to 'info-gdb', or to 'help-gdb', or to any newsgroups.** Most users of GDB do not want to receive bug reports. Those that do, have arranged to receive 'bug-gdb'.

The mailing list 'bug-gdb' has a newsgroup 'gnu.gdb.bug' which serves as a repeater. The mailing list and the newsgroup carry exactly the same messages. Often people think of posting bug reports to the newsgroup instead of mailing them. This appears to work, but it has one problem which can be crucial: a newsgroup posting often lacks a mail path back to the sender. Thus, if we need to ask for more information, we may be unable to reach you. For this reason, it is better to send bug reports to the mailing list.

As a last resort, send bug reports on paper to:

```
GNU Debugger Bugs
Free Software Foundation
545 Tech Square
Cambridge, MA 02139
```

The fundamental principle of reporting bugs usefully is this: **report all the facts**. If you are not sure whether to state a fact or leave it out, state it!

Often people omit facts because they think they know what causes the problem and assume that some details do not matter. Thus, you might assume that the name of the variable you use in an example does not matter. Well, probably it does not, but one cannot be sure. Perhaps the bug is a stray memory reference which happens to fetch from the location where that name is stored in memory; perhaps, if the name were different, the contents of that location would fool the debugger into doing the right thing despite the bug. Play it safe and give a specific, complete example. That is the easiest thing for you to do, and the most helpful.

Keep in mind that the purpose of a bug report is to enable us to fix the bug if it is new to us. It is not as important as what happens if the bug is already known. Therefore, always write your bug reports on the assumption that the bug has not been reported previously.

Sometimes people give a few sketchy facts and ask, "Does this ring a bell?" Those bug reports are useless, and we urge everyone to *refuse to respond to them* except to chide the sender to report bugs properly.

To enable us to fix the bug, you should include all these things:

- The version of GDB. GDB announces it if you start with no arguments; you can also print it at any time using show version.

  Without this, we will not know whether there is any point in looking for the bug in the current version of GDB.

- The type of machine you are using, and the operating system name and version number.

- What compiler (and its version) was used to compile GDB—e.g. "gcc-

1.37.1".

- What compiler (and its version) was used to compile the program you are debugging—e.g. "gcc-1.37.1".

- The command arguments you gave the compiler to compile your example and observe the bug. For example, did you use '-O'? To guarantee you will not omit something important, list them all. A copy of the Makefile (or the output from make) is sufficient.

  If we were to try to guess the arguments, we would probably guess wrong and then we might not encounter the bug.

- A complete input script, and all necessary source files, that will reproduce the bug.

- A description of what behavior you observe that you believe is incorrect. For example, "It gets a fatal signal."

  Of course, if the bug is that GDB gets a fatal signal, then we will certainly notice it. But if the bug is incorrect output, we might not notice unless it is glaringly wrong. We are human, after all. You might as well not give us a chance to make a mistake.

  Even if the problem you experience is a fatal signal, you should still say so explicitly. Suppose something strange is going on, such as, your copy of GDB is out of synch, or you have encountered a bug in the C library on your system. (This has happened!) Your copy might crash and ours would not. If you told us to expect a crash, then when ours fails to crash, we would know that the bug was not happening for us. If you had not told us to expect a crash, then we would not be able to draw any conclusion from our observations.

- If you wish to suggest changes to the GDB source, send us context diffs. If you even discuss something in the GDB source, refer to it by context, not by line number.

  The line numbers in our development sources will not match those in your sources. Your line numbers would convey no useful information to us.

Here are some things that are not necessary:

- A description of the envelope of the bug.

  Often people who encounter a bug spend a lot of time investigating which changes to the input file will make the bug go away and which changes will not affect it.

  This is often time consuming and not very useful, because the way we will find the bug is by running a single example under the debugger with breakpoints, not by pure deduction from a series of examples. We recommend that you save your time for something else.

Of course, if you can find a simpler example to report *instead* of the original one, that is a convenience for us. Errors in the output will be easier to spot, running under the debugger will take less time, etc.

However, simplification is not vital; if you do not want to do this, report the bug anyway and send us the entire test case you used.

- A patch for the bug.

A patch for the bug does help us if it is a good one. But do not omit the necessary information, such as the test case, on the assumption that a patch is all we need. We might see problems with your patch and decide to fix the problem another way, or we might not understand it at all.

Sometimes with a program as complicated as GDB it is very hard to construct an example that will make the program follow a certain path through the code. If you do not send us the example, we will not be able to construct one, so we will not be able to verify that the bug is fixed.

And if we cannot understand what bug you are trying to fix, or why your patch should be an improvement, we will not install it. A test case will help us to understand.

- A guess about what the bug is or what it depends on.

Such guesses are usually wrong. Even we cannot guess right about such things without first using the debugger to find the facts.

# Appendix A  Command Line Editing

This appendix describes GNU's command line editing interface. Often during an interactive session you will type in a long line of text, only to notice that the first word on the line is misspelled. The Readline library gives you a set of commands for manipulating the text as you type it in, allowing you to just fix your typo, and not forcing you to retype the majority of the line. Using these editing commands, you move the cursor to the place that needs correction, and delete or insert the text of the corrections. Then, when you are satisfied with the line, you simply press RETURN. You do not have to be at the end of the line to press RETURN; the entire line will be accepted in any case.

## A.1  Conventions on Notation

In this Appendix, the following notation is used to describe keystrokes.

The text C-k is read as 'Control-K' and describes the character produced when the Control key is depressed and the K key is struck.

The text M-k is read as 'Meta-K' and describes the character produced when the meta key (if you have one) is depressed, and the K key is struck. If you do not have a meta key, it is equivalent to type ESC first, and then type K. Either process is known as *metafying* the K key.

The text M-C-k is read as 'Meta-Control-k' and describes the character produced by *metafying* C-k.

In addition, several keys have their own names. Specifically, DEL, ESC, LFD, SPC, RET, and TAB all stand for themselves when seen in this text, or in an init file (see Section A.3 [Readline Init File], page 134, for more info).

## A.2  Readline Interaction

You need to know very little to start using Readline; as you become more expert, you can do more and more.

### A.2.1  Bare Essentials

In order to enter characters into the line, simply type them. The typed character appears where the cursor was, and then the cursor moves one space to the right. If you mistype a character, you can use DEL to back up, and delete the mistyped character.

Sometimes you may miss typing a character that you wanted to type, and not notice your error until you have typed several other characters. In that case, you can type C-b to move the cursor to the left, and then correct your mistake. Aftwerwards, you can move the cursor to the right with C-f.

When you add text in the middle of a line, you will notice that characters to the right of the cursor get 'pushed over' to make room for the text that you have inserted. Likewise, when you delete text behind the cursor, characters to the right of the cursor get 'pulled back' to fill in the blank space created by the removal of the text. A list of the basic bare essentials for editing the text of an input line follows.

C-b          Move back one character.

C-f          Move forward one character.

DEL          Delete the character to the left of the cursor.

C-d          Delete the character underneath the cursor.

c            Insert an ordinary printing character c into the line at the cursor.

C-_          Undo the last thing that you did. You can undo all the way back to an empty line.

## A.2.2  Movement Commands

The above table describes the most basic possible keystrokes that you need in order to do editing of the input line. For your convenience, many other commands have been added in addition to C-b, C-f, C-d, and DEL. Here are some commands for moving more rapidly about the line.

C-a          Move to the start of the line.

C-e          Move to the end of the line.

M-f          Move forward a word.

M-b          Move backward a word.

C-l          Clear the screen, reprinting the current line at the top.

Notice how C-f moves forward a character, while M-f moves forward a word. It is a loose convention that control keystrokes operate on characters while meta keystrokes operate on words.

## A.2.3  Killing Commands

*Killing* text means to delete the text from the line, but to save it away for later use, usually by *yanking* it back into the line. If the description for a command says that it 'kills' text, then you can be sure that you can get the text back in a different (or the same) place later.

Here is the list of commands for killing text.

C-k       Kill the text from the current cursor position to the end of the line.

M-d       Kill from the cursor to the end of the current word, or if between words, to the end of the next word.

M-DEL     Kill from the cursor the start ofthe previous word, or if between words, to the start of the previous word.

C-w       Kill from the cursor to the previous whitespace. This is different than M-DEL because the word boundaries differ.

And, here is how to *yank* the text back into the line. The yanks commands are:

C-y       Yank the most recently killed text back into the buffer at the cursor.

M-y       Rotate the kill-ring, and yank the new top. You can only do this if the prior command is C-y or M-y.

When you use a kill command, the text is saved in a *kill-ring*. Any number of consecutive kills save all of the killed text together, so that when you yank it back, you get it in one clean sweep. The kill ring is not line specific; the text that you killed on a previously typed line is available to be yanked back later, when you are typing another line.

## A.2.4 Arguments

You can pass numeric arguments to Readline commands. Sometimes the argument acts as a repeat count, other times it is the *sign* of the argument that is significant. If you pass a negative argument to a command which normally acts in a forward direction, that command will act in a backward direction. For example, to kill text back to the start of the line, you might type M-- C-k.

The general way to pass numeric arguments to a command is to type meta digits before the command. If the first 'digit' you type is a minus sign (-), then the sign of the argument will be negative. Once you have typed one meta digit to get the argument started, you can type the remainder of the digits, and then the command. For example, to give the C-d command an argument of 10, you could type M-1 0 C-d.

## A.3 Readline Init File

Although the Readline library comes with a set of Emacs-like keybindings, it is possible that you would like to use a different set of keybindings. You can customize programs that use Readline by putting commands in an *init* file in your home directory. The name of this file is '`~/.inputrc`'.

When a program which uses the Readline library starts up, it reads the file '`~/.inputrc`', and sets the keybindings.

### A.3.1 Readline Init Syntax

You can start up with a vi-like editing mode by placing

```
set editing-mode vi
```

in your '`~/.inputrc`' file.

You can have Readline use a single line for display, scrolling the input between the two edges of the screen by placing

```
set horizontal-scroll-mode On
```

in your '`~/.inputrc`' file.

The syntax for controlling keybindings in the '`~/.inputrc`' file is simple. First you have to know the *name* of the command that you want to change. The following pages contain tables of the command name, the default keybinding, and a short description of what the command does.

Once you know the name of the command, simply place the name of the key you wish to bind the command to, a colon, and then the name of the command on a line in the '`~/.inputrc`' file. Here is an example:

```
# This is a comment line.
Meta-Rubout:  backward-kill-word
Control-u:  universal-argument
```

### A.3.1.1 Moving

Here are commands for moving the cursor:

`beginning-of-line (C-a)`

　　　　Move to the start of the current line.

`end-of-line (C-e)`

　　　　Move to the end of the line.

`forward-char (C-f)`

　　　　Move forward a character.

`backward-char (C-b)`

> Move back a character.

`forward-word (M-f)`

> Move forward to the end of the next word.

`backward-word (M-b)`

> Move back to the start of this, or the previous, word.

`clear-screen (C-l)`

> Clear the screen leaving the current line at the top of the screen.

## A.3.1.2  Using the History

Here are commands for using the history:

`accept-line (Newline, Return)`

> Accept the line regardless of where the cursor is. If this line is non-empty, add it to the history list. If this line was a history line, then restore the history line to its original state.

`previous-history (C-p)`

> Move 'up' through the history list.

`next-history (C-n)`

> Move 'down' through the history list.

`beginning-of-history (M-<)`

> Move to the first line in the history.

`end-of-history (M->)`

> Move to the end of the input history, i.e., the line you are entering!

`reverse-search-history (C-r)`

> Search backward starting at the current line and moving 'up' through the history as necessary. This is an incremental search.

`forward-search-history (C-s)`

> Search forward starting at the current line and moving 'down' through the the history as neccessary.

## A.3.1.3  Changing Text

Here are commands for changing text:

`delete-char (C-d)`

> Delete the character under the cursor. If the cursor is at the beginning of the line, and there are no characters in the line, and the last character typed was not C-d, then return EOF.

`backward-delete-char (Rubout)`

> Delete the character behind the cursor. A numeric arg says to kill the characters instead of deleting them.

`quoted-insert (C-q, C-v)`

> Add the next character that you type to the line verbatim. This is how to insert things like C-q, for example.

`tab-insert (M-TAB)`

> Insert a tab character.

`self-insert (a, b, A, 1, !, ...)`

> Insert an ordinary printing character into the line.

`transpose-chars (C-t)`

> Drag the character before point forward over the character at point. Point moves forward as well. If point is at the end of the line, then transpose the two characters before point. Negative args don't work.

`transpose-words (M-t)`

> Drag the word behind the cursor past the word in front of the cursor moving the cursor over that word as well.

`upcase-word (M-u)`

> Uppercase the current (or following) word. With a negative argument, do the previous word, but do not move point.

`downcase-word (M-l)`

> Lowercase the current (or following) word. With a negative argument, do the previous word, but do not move point.

`capitalize-word (M-c)`

> Uppercase the current (or following) word. With a negative argument, do the previous word, but do not move point.

### A.3.1.4 Killing and Yanking

Here are commands for removing text and getting it back:

`kill-line (C-k)`

> Kill the text from the current cursor position to the end of the line.

`backward-kill-line ()`

> Kill backward to the beginning of the line. This is normally unbound.

`kill-word (M-d)`

> Kill from the cursor to the end of the current word, or if between words, to the end of the next word.

`backward-kill-word (M-DEL)`

> Kill the word behind the cursor.

`unix-line-discard (C-u)`

> Kill the entire line. This is similar to the use of the Unix kill character (often also C-U), save that here the killed text can be retrieved later (since it goes on the kill-ring).

`unix-word-rubout (C-w)`

> Kill the current word, like the Unix word erase character. The killed text goes on the kill-ring. This is different than `backward-kill-word` because the word boundaries differ.

`yank (C-y)`

> Yank the top of the kill ring into the buffer at point.

`yank-pop (M-y)`

> Rotate the kill-ring, and yank the new top. You can only do this if the prior command is `yank` or `yank-pop`.

## A.3.1.5 Numeric Arguments

> Here are commands for providing Readline commands with numeric arguments:

`digit-argument (M-0, M-1, ... M--)`

> Add this digit to the argument already accumulating, or start a new argument. `M--` starts a negative argument.

`universal-argument ()`

> Do what `C-u` does in Emacs. By default, this is not bound to any keys.

## A.3.1.6 Letting Readline Type

> Here are commands that save typing:

complete (TAB)

>Attempt to do completion on the text before point. This is implementation defined. Generally, if you are typing a filename argument, you can do filename completion; if you are typing a command, you can do command completion, if you are typing in a symbol to GDB, you can do symbol name completion, if you are typing in a variable to Bash, you can do variable name completion...

possible-completions (M-?)

>List the possible completions of the text before point.

### A.3.1.7 Other Commands

Here are commands for canceling commands and for undoing actions, among others:

abort (C-g)

>The line editing commands reverse-search-history (C-r) and forward-search-history (C-s) go into a separate input mode; you can abort the search, and return to normal input mode, by using the abort (C-g) command.

do-uppercase-version (M-a, M-b, ...)

>Run the command that is bound to your uppercase brother.

prefix-meta (ESC)

>Make the next character that you type be metafied. This is for people without a meta key. ESC-f is equivalent to M-f.

undo (C-_)

>Incremental undo, separately remembered for each line.

revert-line (M-r)

>Undo all changes made to this line. This is like typing the 'undo' command enough times to get back to the beginning.

### A.3.2 Readline vi Mode

While the Readline library does not have a full set of vi editing functions, it does contain enough to allow simple editing of the line.

In order to switch interactively between Emacs and vi editing modes, use the command M-C-j (toggle-editing-mode).

When you enter a line in vi mode, you are already in "insertion" mode, as if you had typed an i. Pressing ESC switches you into "edit" mode, where you can edit the text of the line with the standard vi movement keys, move to previous history lines with k, to following lines with j, and so forth.

# Appendix B  Command Line History

This Appendix describes the GNU History library, a programming tool that provides a consistent user interface for recalling lines of previously typed input.

## B.1  Introduction to History

Many programs read input from the user a line at a time. The GNU history library is able to keep track of those lines, associate arbitrary data with each line, and utilize information from previous lines in making up new ones.

The programmer using the History library has available to him functions for remembering lines on a history stack, associating arbitrary data with a line, removing lines from the stack, searching through the stack for a line containing an arbitrary text string, and referencing any line on the stack directly. In addition, a history *expansion* function is available which provides for a consistent user interface across many different programs.

When you use programs written with the History library, you have the benefit of a consistent user interface, with a set of well-known commands for manipulating the text of previous lines and using that text in new commands. The basic history manipulation commands are similar to the history substitution used by `csh`.

GNU programs often also use the Readline library, which includes history manipulation by default, and has the added advantage of Emacs style command line editing.

## B.2  History Interaction

The History library provides a history expansion feature that is similar to the history expansion in `csh`. The following text describes what syntax features are available.

History expansion takes place in two parts. The first is to determine which line from the previous history should be used during substitution. The second is to select portions of that line for inclusion into the current one. The line selected from the previous history is called the *event*, and the portions of that line that are acted upon are called *words*. The line is broken into words in the same fashion used by the Bash shell, so that several words surrounded by quotes are treated as if they were a single word.

## B.2.1  Event Designators

An event designator is a reference to a command line entry in the history list.

| | |
|---|---|
| ! | Start a history subsititution, except when followed by a space, tab, or the end of the line; or by '=' or '('. |
| !! | Refer to the previous command. This is a synonym for !-1. |
| !*n* | Refer to command line *n*. |
| !-*n* | Refer to the command line *n* lines back. |
| !*string* | Refer to the most recent command starting with *string*. |
| !?*string*[?] | |
| | Refer to the most recent command containing *string*. |

## B.2.2  Word Designators

A ':' separates the event specification from the word designator. It can be omitted if the word designator begins with a '^', '$', '*' or '%'. Words are numbered from the beginning of the line, with the first word being denoted by a 0 (zero).

| | |
|---|---|
| 0 (zero) | The zero'th word. For many applications, this is the command word. |
| n | The *n*'th word. |
| ^ | The first argument. that is, word 1. |
| $ | The last argument. |
| % | The word matched by the most recent ?*string*? search. |
| *x-y* | A range of words; -*y* abbreviates 0-*y*. |
| * | All of the words, excepting the zero'th. This is a synonym for '1-$'. It is not an error to use '*' if there is just one word in the event. The empty string is returned in that case. |

## B.2.3  Modifiers

After the optional word designator, you can add a sequence of one or more of the following modifiers, each preceded by a ':'.

| | |
|---|---|
| # | The entire command line typed so far. This means the current command, not the previous command, so it really isn't a word designator, and doesn't belong in this section. |
| h | Remove a trailing pathname component, leaving only the head. |

r    Remove a trailing suffix of the form '.*suffix*', leaving the base-
     name.

e    Remove all but the suffix.

t    Remove all leading pathname components, leaving the tail.

p    Print the new command but do not execute it. This takes effect
     immediately, so it should be the last specifier on the line.

# Appendix C  Renamed Commands

The following commands were renamed in GDB 4, in order to make the command set as a whole more consistent and easier to use and remember:

| Old Command | New Command |
| --- | --- |
| add-syms | add-symbol-file |
| delete environment | unset environment |
| info convenience | show convenience |
| info copying | show copying |
| info directories | show directories |
| info editing | show commands |
| info history | show values |
| info targets | help target |
| info values | show values |
| info version | show version |
| info warranty | show warranty |
| set/ show addressprint | set/ show print address |
| set/ show array-max | set/ show print elements |
| set/ show arrayprint | set/ show print array |
| set/ show asm-demangle | set/ show print asm-demangle |
| set/ show caution | set/ show confirm |
| set/ show demangle | set/ show print demangle |
| set/ show history write | set/ show history save |
| set/ show prettyprint | set/ show print pretty |
| set/ show screen-height | set/ show height |
| set/ show screen-width | set/ show width |
| set/ show sevenbit-strings | set/ show print sevenbit-strings |
| set/ show unionprint | set/ show print union |
| set/ show vtblprint | set/ show print vtbl |
| | |
| unset | (No longer an alias for delete) |

# Appendix D  Installing GDB

GDB comes with a `configure` script that automates the process of preparing GDB for installation; you can then use **make** to build the **gdb** program.[1]

The GDB distribution includes all the source code you need for GDB in a single directory, whose name is usually composed by appending the version number to 'gdb'.

For example, the GDB Version 4.3 distribution is in the 'gdb-4.3' directory. That directory contains:

gdb-4.3/configure (and supporting files)
> script for configuring GDB and all its supporting libraries.

gdb-4.3/gdb
> the source specific to GDB itself

gdb-4.3/bfd
> source for the Binary File Descriptor Library

gdb-4.3/include
> GNU include files

gdb-4.3/libiberty
> source for the '-liberty' free software library

gdb-4.3/readline
> source for the GNU command-line interface

The simplest way to configure and build GDB is to run `configure` from the 'gdb-*version-number*' source directory, which in this example is the 'gdb-4.3' directory.

First switch to the 'gdb-*version-number*' source directory if you are not already in it; then run `configure`. Pass the identifier for the platform on which GDB will run as an argument.

For example:

```
cd gdb-4.3
./configure host
make
```

---

[1] If you have a more recent version of GDB than 4.3, look at the 'README' file in the sources; we may have improved the installation procedures since publishing this manual.

where *host* is an identifier such as 'sun4' or 'decstation', that identifies the platform where GDB will run.

This `configure` command builds the three libraries 'bfd', 'readline', and 'libiberty', then gdb itself. The configured source files, and the binaries, are left in the corresponding source directories.

`configure` is a Bourne-shell (`/bin/sh`) script; if your system does not recognize this automatically when you run a different shell, you may need to run `sh` on it explicitly:

    sh configure *host*

You can *run* the `configure` script from any of the subordinate directories in the GDB distribution, if you only want to configure that subdirectory; but be sure to specify a path to it.

For example, with version 4.3, type the following to configure only the bfd subdirectory:

    cd gdb-4.3/bfd
    ../configure *host*

You can install gdb anywhere; it has no hardwired paths. However, you should make sure that the shell on your path (named by the 'SHELL' environment variable) is publicly readable. Remember that GDB uses the shell to start your program—some systems refuse to let GDB debug child processes whose programs are not readable.

## D.1  Configuration Subdirectories

If you want to run GDB versions for several host or target machines, you'll need a different gdb compiled for each combination of host and target. `configure` is designed to make this easy by allowing you to generate each configuration in a separate subdirectory. If your make program handles the 'VPATH' feature (GNU make does), then running make in each of these directories builds the gdb program specified there.

`configure` creates these subdirectories for you when you simultaneously specify several configurations; but it is a good habit even for a single configuration. You can specify the use of subdirectories using the '--subdirs' option (abbreviated '--sub').

For example, with version 4.3, you can build GDB on a Sun 4 like this:

```
cd gdb-4.3
./configure --sub sun4
cd H-sun4/T-sun4
make
```

When `configure` uses subdirectories to build programs or libraries, it creates nested directories 'H-*host*/T-*target*'. `configure` uses these two directory levels because GDB can be configured for cross-compiling: GDB can run on one machine (the host) while debugging programs that run on another machine (the target). You specify cross-debugging targets by giving the '`--target=`*target*' option to `configure`. Specifying only hosts still gives you two levels of subdirectory for each host, with the same configuration suffix on both; that is, if you give any number of hosts but no targets, GDB will be configured for native debugging on each host. On the other hand, whenever you specify both hosts and targets on the same command line, `configure` creates all combinations of the hosts and targets you list.

If you run `configure` from a directory that contains source directories for multiple libraries or programs, such as the 'gdb-4.3' source directory for version 4.3, `configure` creates the 'H-*host*/T-*target*' subdirectories in each library or program's source directory.

For example, with version 4.3, typing:

```
cd gdb-4.3
configure sun4 --target=vxworks960
```

creates the following directories:

```
gdb-4.3/H-sun4/T-vxworks960
gdb-4.3/bfd/H-sun4/T-vxworks960
gdb-4.3/gdb/H-sun4/T-vxworks960
gdb-4.3/libiberty/H-sun4/T-vxworks960
gdb-4.3/readline/H-sun4/T-vxworks960
```

When you run `make` to build a program or library, you must run it in a configured directory. If you made a single configuration, without subdirectories, run `make` in the source directory. If you have 'H-*host*/T-*target*' subdirectories, run `make` in those subdirectories.

The `Makefile` generated by `configure` for each source directory runs recursively. Thus, if you type `make` in a source directory such as 'gdb-4.3' (or in a subdirectory, such as 'gdb-4.3/H-*host*/T-*target*'), you will build all the required libraries, and then build GDB.

When you have multiple hosts or targets configured, you can run `make` on them in parallel (for example, if they are NFS-mounted on each of the hosts); they will not interfere with each other.

You can also use the '`--objdir=`*altroot*' option to have the configured files placed in a parallel directory structure rather than alongside the source files; see Section D.3 [`configure` Options], page 151.

## D.2  Specifying Names for Hosts and Targets

The specifications used for hosts and targets in the `configure` script are based on a three-part naming scheme, but some short predefined aliases are also supported. The full naming scheme encodes three pieces of information in the following pattern:

*architecture-vendor-os*

For example, you can use the alias `sun4` as a *host* argument or in a `--target=target` option, but the equivalent full name is 'sparc-sun-sunos4'.

The following table shows all the architectures, hosts, and OS prefixes that `configure` recognizes in GDB Version 4.3. Entries in the "OS prefix" column ending in a '*' may be followed by a release number.

| Architecture | Vendor | | OS prefix | |
|---|---|---|---|---|
| 580 | altos | hp | aix* | msdos* |
| a29k | amd | ibm | amigados | newsos* |
| alliant | amdahl | intel | aout | nindy* |
| arm | aout | isi | bout | osf* |
| c1 | apollo | little | bsd* | sco* |
| c2 | att | mips | coff | sunos* |
| cray2 | bcs | motorola | ctix* | svr4 |
| h8300 | bout | ncr | dgux* | sym* |
| i386 | bull | next | dynix* | sysv* |
| i860 | cbm | nyu | ebmon | ultrix* |
| i960 | coff | sco | esix* | unicos* |
| m68000 | convergent | sequent | hds | unos* |
| m68k | convex | sgi | hpux* | uts |
| m88k | cray | sony | irix* | v88r* |
| mips | dec | sun | isc* | vms* |
| ns32k | encore | unicom | kern | vxworks* |
| pyramid | gould | utek | mach* | |
| romp | hitachi | wrs | | |
| rs6000 | | | | |
| sparc | | | | |
| tahoe | | | | |
| tron | | | | |
| vax | | | | |
| xmp | | | | |
| ymp | | | | |

*Warning:* `configure` can represent a very large number of combinations of architecture, vendor, and OS. There is by no means support available for all possible combinations!

The `configure` script accompanying GDB does not provide any query facility to list all supported host and target names or aliases. `configure` calls the Bourne shell script `config.sub` to map abbreviations to full names; you can read the script, if you wish, or you can use it to test your guesses on abbreviations—for example:

```
% sh config.sub sun4
sparc-sun-sunos4
% sh config.sub sun3
m68k-sun-sunos4
% sh config.sub decstation
mips-dec-ultrix
% sh config.sub hp300bsd
m68k-hp-bsd
% sh config.sub i386v
i386-none-sysv
% sh config.sub i486v
*** Configuration "i486v" not recognized
```

`config.sub` is also distributed in the GDB source directory (`gdb-4.3`, for version 4.3).

## D.3 `configure` Options

Here is a summary of all the `configure` options and arguments that you might use for building GDB:

```
configure [--destdir=dir] [--subdirs]
          [--objdir=altroot] [--norecursion]
          [--rm]
          [--target=target...] host...
```

You may introduce options with the character '-' rather than '--' if you prefer; but you may abbreviate option names if you use '--'.

`--destdir=dir`

> *dir* is an installation directory *path prefix*. After you configure with this option, `make install` will install GDB as '*dir*/bin/gdb', and the libraries in '*dir*/lib'. If you specify '--destdir=/usr/local', for example, `make install` creates '/usr/local/bin/gdb'.

**--subdirs**

> Write configuration specific files in subdirectories of the form
>
> > H-*host*/T-*target*
>
> (and configure the `Makefile` to generate object code in subdirectories of this form as well). Without this option, if you specify only one configuration for GDB, `configure` will use the same directory for source, configured files, and binaries. This option is used automatically if you specify more than one *host* or more than one '--**target**=*target*' option on the `configure` command line.

**--norecursion**

> Configure only the directory where `configure` is executed; do not propagate configuration to subdirectories.

**--objdir=**a*ltroot*

> *altroot* is an alternative directory used as the root for configured files. `configure` will create directories under *altroot* in parallel to the source directories. If you use '--**objdir**=*altroot*' with '--**subdirs**', `configure` also builds the 'H-*host*/T-*target*' subdirectories in the directory tree rooted in *altroot*.

**--rm**          Remove the configuration that the other arguments specify.

**--target=**target ...

> Configure GDB for cross-debugging programs running on each specified *target*. You may specify as many '--**target**' options as you wish. Without this option, GDB is configured to debug programs that run on the same machine (*host*) as GDB itself.
>
> There is no convenient way to generate a list of all available targets.

*host* ...     Configure GDB to run on each specified *host*. You may specify as many host names as you wish.

> There is no convenient way to generate a list of all available hosts.

`configure` accepts other options, for compatibility with configuring other GNU tools recursively; but these are the only options that affect GDB or its supporting libraries.

## D.4  Formatting the Documentation

All the documentation for GDB, including this manual, comes as part of the distribution. The documentation is written in Texinfo format, which is a documentation system that uses a single source file to produce both on-line information and a printed manual. You can use one of the Info formatting commands to create the on-line version of the documentation and TeX (or `texi2roff`) to typeset the printed version.

GDB includes an already formatted copy of the on-line Info version of this manual in the 'gdb' subdirectory. The main Info file is 'gdb-*version-number*/gdb/gdb.info', and it refers to subordinate files matching 'gdb.info*' in the same directory.

If you want to format these Info files yourself, you need one of the Info formatting programs, such as `texinfo-format-buffer` or `makeinfo`.

If you have `makeinfo` installed, and are in the top level GDB source directory ('gdb-4.3', in the case of version 4.3), you can make the Info file by typing:

```
cd gdb
make gdb.info
```

If you want to typeset and print copies of this manual, you need TeX, a printing program such as `lpr`, and 'texinfo.tex', the Texinfo definitions file.

TeX is a typesetting program; it does not print files directly, but produces output files called DVI files. To print a typeset document, you need a program to print DVI files. If your system has TeX installed, chances are it has such a program. The precise command to use depends on your system; `lpr -d` is common; another is `dvips`. The DVI print command may require a file name without any extension or a '.dvi' extension.

TeX also requires a macro definitions file called 'texinfo.tex'. This file tells TeX how to typeset a document written in Texinfo format. On its own, TeX cannot read, much less typeset a Texinfo file. 'texinfo.tex' is distributed with GDB and is located in the 'gdb-*version-number*/texinfo' directory.

If you have TeX and a DVI printer program installed, you can typeset and print this manual. First switch to the the 'gdb' subdirectory of the main source directory (for example, to 'gdb-4.3/gdb') and then type:

```
make gdb.dvi
```

In addition to the manual, the GDB 4 release includes a three-column reference card. Format the GDB reference card by typing:

```
make refcard.dvi
```

The GDB reference card is designed to print in landscape mode on US "letter" size paper; that is, on a sheet 8.5 inches wide by 11 inches high. You will need to specify this form of printing as an option to your DVI output program.

# GNU GENERAL PUBLIC LICENSE

Version 2, June 1991

Copyright © 1989, 1991 Free Software Foundation, Inc.
675 Mass Ave, Cambridge, MA 02139, USA

## Preamble

The licenses for most software are designed to take away your freedom
to share and change it. By contrast, the GNU General Public License is
intended to guarantee your freedom to share and change free software—to
make sure the software is free for all its users. This General Public License
applies to most of the Free Software Foundation's software and to any other
program whose authors commit to using it. (Some other Free Software
Foundation software is covered by the GNU Library General Public License
instead.) You can apply it to your programs, too.

When we speak of free software, we are referring to freedom, not price.
Our General Public Licenses are designed to make sure that you have the
freedom to distribute copies of free software (and charge for this service if
you wish), that you receive source code or can get it if you want it, that you
can change the software or use pieces of it in new free programs; and that
you know you can do these things.

To protect your rights, we need to make restrictions that forbid anyone to
deny you these rights or to ask you to surrender the rights. These restrictions
translate to certain responsibilities for you if you distribute copies of the
software, or if you modify it.

For example, if you distribute copies of such a program, whether gratis
or for a fee, you must give the recipients all the rights that you have. You
must make sure that they, too, receive or can get the source code. And you
must show them these terms so they know their rights.

We protect your rights with two steps: (1) copyright the software, and
(2) offer you this license which gives you legal permission to copy, distribute
and/or modify the software.

Also, for each author's protection and ours, we want to make certain
that everyone understands that there is no warranty for this free software.
If the software is modified by someone else and passed on, we want its recip-

ients to know that what they have is not the original, so that any problems introduced by others will not reflect on the original authors' reputations.

Finally, any free program is threatened constantly by software patents. We wish to avoid the danger that redistributors of a free program will individually obtain patent licenses, in effect making the program proprietary. To prevent this, we have made it clear that any patent must be licensed for everyone's free use or not licensed at all.

The precise terms and conditions for copying, distribution and modification follow.

# TERMS AND CONDITIONS

1. This License applies to any program or other work which contains a notice placed by the copyright holder saying it may be distributed under the terms of this General Public License. The "Program", below, refers to any such program or work, and a "work based on the Program" means either the Program or any derivative work under copyright law: that is to say, a work containing the Program or a portion of it, either verbatim or with modifications and/or translated into another language. (Hereinafter, translation is included without limitation in the term "modification".) Each licensee is addressed as "you".

   Activities other than copying, distribution and modification are not covered by this License; they are outside its scope. The act of running the Program is not restricted, and the output from the Program is covered only if its contents constitute a work based on the Program (independent of having been made by running the Program). Whether that is true depends on what the Program does.

2. You may copy and distribute verbatim copies of the Program's source code as you receive it, in any medium, provided that you conspicuously and appropriately publish on each copy an appropriate copyright notice and disclaimer of warranty; keep intact all the notices that refer to this License and to the absence of any warranty; and give any other recipients of the Program a copy of this License along with the Program.

   You may charge a fee for the physical act of transferring a copy, and you may at your option offer warranty protection in exchange for a fee.

3. You may modify your copy or copies of the Program or any portion of it, thus forming a work based on the Program, and copy and distribute such modifications or work under the terms of Section 1 above, provided that you also meet all of these conditions:

a. You must cause the modified files to carry prominent notices stating that you changed the files and the date of any change.

b. You must cause any work that you distribute or publish, that in whole or in part contains or is derived from the Program or any part thereof, to be licensed as a whole at no charge to all third parties under the terms of this License.

c. If the modified program normally reads commands interactively when run, you must cause it, when started running for such interactive use in the most ordinary way, to print or display an announcement including an appropriate copyright notice and a notice that there is no warranty (or else, saying that you provide a warranty) and that users may redistribute the program under these conditions, and telling the user how to view a copy of this License. (Exception: if the Program itself is interactive but does not normally print such an announcement, your work based on the Program is not required to print an announcement.)

These requirements apply to the modified work as a whole. If identifiable sections of that work are not derived from the Program, and can be reasonably considered independent and separate works in themselves, then this License, and its terms, do not apply to those sections when you distribute them as separate works. But when you distribute the same sections as part of a whole which is a work based on the Program, the distribution of the whole must be on the terms of this License, whose permissions for other licensees extend to the entire whole, and thus to each and every part regardless of who wrote it.

Thus, it is not the intent of this section to claim rights or contest your rights to work written entirely by you; rather, the intent is to exercise the right to control the distribution of derivative or collective works based on the Program.

In addition, mere aggregation of another work not based on the Program with the Program (or with a work based on the Program) on a volume of a storage or distribution medium does not bring the other work under the scope of this License.

4. You may copy and distribute the Program (or a work based on it, under Section 2) in object code or executable form under the terms of Sections 1 and 2 above provided that you also do one of the following:

a. Accompany it with the complete corresponding machine-readable source code, which must be distributed under the terms of Sections 1 and 2 above on a medium customarily used for software interchange; or,

b. Accompany it with a written offer, valid for at least three years, to give any third party, for a charge no more than your cost of physically performing source distribution, a complete machine-readable copy of the corresponding source code, to be distributed under the terms of Sections 1 and 2 above on a medium customarily used for software interchange; or,

c. Accompany it with the information you received as to the offer to distribute corresponding source code. (This alternative is allowed only for noncommercial distribution and only if you received the program in object code or executable form with such an offer, in accord with Subsection b above.)

The source code for a work means the preferred form of the work for making modifications to it. For an executable work, complete source code means all the source code for all modules it contains, plus any associated interface definition files, plus the scripts used to control compilation and installation of the executable. However, as a special exception, the source code distributed need not include anything that is normally distributed (in either source or binary form) with the major components (compiler, kernel, and so on) of the operating system on which the executable runs, unless that component itself accompanies the executable.

If distribution of executable or object code is made by offering access to copy from a designated place, then offering equivalent access to copy the source code from the same place counts as distribution of the source code, even though third parties are not compelled to copy the source along with the object code.

5. You may not copy, modify, sublicense, or distribute the Program except as expressly provided under this License. Any attempt otherwise to copy, modify, sublicense or distribute the Program is void, and will automatically terminate your rights under this License. However, parties who have received copies, or rights, from you under this License will not have their licenses terminated so long as such parties remain in full compliance.

6. You are not required to accept this License, since you have not signed it. However, nothing else grants you permission to modify or distribute the Program or its derivative works. These actions are prohibited by law if you do not accept this License. Therefore, by modifying or distributing the Program (or any work based on the Program), you indicate your acceptance of this License to do so, and all its terms and conditions for copying, distributing or modifying the Program or works based on it.

7. Each time you redistribute the Program (or any work based on the

Program), the recipient automatically receives a license from the original licensor to copy, distribute or modify the Program subject to these terms and conditions. You may not impose any further restrictions on the recipients' exercise of the rights granted herein. You are not responsible for enforcing compliance by third parties to this License.

8. If, as a consequence of a court judgment or allegation of patent infringement or for any other reason (not limited to patent issues), conditions are imposed on you (whether by court order, agreement or otherwise) that contradict the conditions of this License, they do not excuse you from the conditions of this License. If you cannot distribute so as to satisfy simultaneously your obligations under this License and any other pertinent obligations, then as a consequence you may not distribute the Program at all. For example, if a patent license would not permit royalty-free redistribution of the Program by all those who receive copies directly or indirectly through you, then the only way you could satisfy both it and this License would be to refrain entirely from distribution of the Program.

   If any portion of this section is held invalid or unenforceable under any particular circumstance, the balance of the section is intended to apply and the section as a whole is intended to apply in other circumstances.

   It is not the purpose of this section to induce you to infringe any patents or other property right claims or to contest validity of any such claims; this section has the sole purpose of protecting the integrity of the free software distribution system, which is implemented by public license practices. Many people have made generous contributions to the wide range of software distributed through that system in reliance on consistent application of that system; it is up to the author/donor to decide if he or she is willing to distribute software through any other system and a licensee cannot impose that choice.

   This section is intended to make thoroughly clear what is believed to be a consequence of the rest of this License.

9. If the distribution and/or use of the Program is restricted in certain countries either by patents or by copyrighted interfaces, the original copyright holder who places the Program under this License may add an explicit geographical distribution limitation excluding those countries, so that distribution is permitted only in or among countries not thus excluded. In such case, this License incorporates the limitation as if written in the body of this License.

10. The Free Software Foundation may publish revised and/or new versions of the General Public License from time to time. Such new versions will be similar in spirit to the present version, but may differ in detail to

address new problems or concerns.

Each version is given a distinguishing version number. If the Program specifies a version number of this License which applies to it and "any later version", you have the option of following the terms and conditions either of that version or of any later version published by the Free Software Foundation. If the Program does not specify a version number of this License, you may choose any version ever published by the Free Software Foundation.

11. If you wish to incorporate parts of the Program into other free programs whose distribution conditions are different, write to the author to ask for permission. For software which is copyrighted by the Free Software Foundation, write to the Free Software Foundation; we sometimes make exceptions for this. Our decision will be guided by the two goals of preserving the free status of all derivatives of our free software and of promoting the sharing and reuse of software generally.

## NO WARRANTY

12. BECAUSE THE PROGRAM IS LICENSED FREE OF CHARGE, THERE IS NO WARRANTY FOR THE PROGRAM, TO THE EXTENT PERMITTED BY APPLICABLE LAW. EXCEPT WHEN OTHERWISE STATED IN WRITING THE COPYRIGHT HOLDERS AND/OR OTHER PARTIES PROVIDE THE PROGRAM "AS IS" WITHOUT WARRANTY OF ANY KIND, EITHER EXPRESSED OR IMPLIED, INCLUDING, BUT NOT LIMITED TO, THE IMPLIED WARRANTIES OF MERCHANTABILITY AND FITNESS FOR A PARTICULAR PURPOSE. THE ENTIRE RISK AS TO THE QUALITY AND PERFORMANCE OF THE PROGRAM IS WITH YOU. SHOULD THE PROGRAM PROVE DEFECTIVE, YOU ASSUME THE COST OF ALL NECESSARY SERVICING, REPAIR OR CORRECTION.

13. IN NO EVENT UNLESS REQUIRED BY APPLICABLE LAW OR AGREED TO IN WRITING WILL ANY COPYRIGHT HOLDER, OR ANY OTHER PARTY WHO MAY MODIFY AND/OR REDISTRIBUTE THE PROGRAM AS PERMITTED ABOVE, BE LIABLE TO YOU FOR DAMAGES, INCLUDING ANY GENERAL, SPECIAL, INCIDENTAL OR CONSEQUENTIAL DAMAGES ARISING OUT OF THE USE OR INABILITY TO USE THE PROGRAM (INCLUDING BUT NOT LIMITED TO LOSS OF DATA OR DATA BEING RENDERED INACCURATE OR LOSSES SUSTAINED BY YOU OR

THIRD PARTIES OR A FAILURE OF THE PROGRAM TO OPER-
ATE WITH ANY OTHER PROGRAMS), EVEN IF SUCH HOLDER
OR OTHER PARTY HAS BEEN ADVISED OF THE POSSIBILITY
OF SUCH DAMAGES.

## END OF TERMS AND CONDITIONS

# Applying These Terms to Your New Programs

If you develop a new program, and you want it to be of the greatest possible use to the public, the best way to achieve this is to make it free software which everyone can redistribute and change under these terms.

To do so, attach the following notices to the program. It is safest to attach them to the start of each source file to most effectively convey the exclusion of warranty; and each file should have at least the "copyright" line and a pointer to where the full notice is found.

```
one line to give the program's name and an idea of what it does.
Copyright (C) 19yy   name of author


This program is free software; you can redistribute it and/or
modify it under the terms of the GNU General Public License
as published by the Free Software Foundation; either version 2
of the License, or (at your option) any later version.


This program is distributed in the hope that it will be useful,
but WITHOUT ANY WARRANTY; without even the implied warranty of
MERCHANTABILITY or FITNESS FOR A PARTICULAR PURPOSE.  See the
GNU General Public License for more details.


You should have received a copy of the GNU General Public License
along with this program; if not, write to the
Free Software Foundation, Inc., 675 Mass Ave,
Cambridge, MA 02139, USA.
```

Also add information on how to contact you by electronic and paper mail.

If the program is interactive, make it output a short notice like this when it starts in an interactive mode:

```
Gnomovision version 69, Copyright (C) 19yy  name of author
Gnomovision comes with ABSOLUTELY NO WARRANTY; for details
type 'show w'.  This is free software, and you are welcome
to redistribute it under certain conditions; type 'show c'
for details.
```

The hypothetical commands 'show w' and 'show c' should show the appropriate parts of the General Public License. Of course, the commands you use may be called something other than 'show w' and 'show c'; they could even be mouse-clicks or menu items—whatever suits your program.

You should also get your employer (if you work as a programmer) or your school, if any, to sign a "copyright disclaimer" for the program, if necessary.

Here is a sample; alter the names:

```
Yoyodyne, Inc., hereby disclaims all copyright
interest in the program 'Gnomovision'
(which makes passes at compilers) written
by James Hacker.
```

*signature of Ty Coon*, 1 April 1989
Ty Coon, President of Vice

This General Public License does not permit incorporating your program into proprietary programs. If your program is a subroutine library, you may consider it more useful to permit linking proprietary applications with the library. If this is what you want to do, use the GNU Library General Public License instead of this License.

# Index

Index

The body of this manual is set in
cmr10 at 10.95pt,
with headings in **cmb10 at 10.95pt**
and examples in `cmtt10 at 10.95pt.`
*cmti10 at 10.95pt,*
**cmb10 at 10.95pt**, and
*cmsl10 at 10.95pt*
are used for emphasis.